NARRATIVES AND FICTIONS IN EDUCATIONAL RESEARCH

Peter Clough

Open University Press
Buckingham · Philadelphia

Open University Press
Celtic Court
22 Ballmoor
Buckingham
MK18 1XW

email: enquiries@openup.co.uk
world wide web: www.openup.co.uk

and
325 Chestnut Street
Philadelphia, PA 19106, USA

First Published 2002

A catalogue record of this book is available from the British Library

ISBN   0 335 20791 X (pb)   0 335 20792 8 (hb)

Library of Congress Cataloging-in-Publication Data
Clough, Peter, 1949–
    Narratives and fictions in educational research/Peter Clough.
        p. cm – (Doing qualitative research in educational settings)
    Includes bibliographical references (p.) and index.
    ISBN 0-335-20792-8 – ISBN 0-335-20791-X (pbk.)
    1. Education–Research. 2. Narration (Rhetoric). 3. Postmodernism and education. I. Title. II. Series.

LB1028.C553   2002
370′7′2–dc21   2001059314

Typeset by Type Study, Scarborough
Printed and bound in Great Britain by Marston Book Services Limited, Oxford

For David Jack Clough

Contents

Series editor's preface

I had never realized just how fascinating research was in its own right. I was expecting the research methods course to be boring, difficult and all about statistics but I couldn't have been more wrong. There is so much to consider, so many aspects, so many ways of finding out what's going on, and not just one way of representing it too. I have really been surprised.

(Student taking an MA in Educational Studies)

I never knew that there was so much to research. I thought that you just chose a method, applied it, did your statistical sums and came up with your findings. The reality is more complicated but so much more interesting and meaningful.

(Student taking an MA in Educational Studies)

The best thing for me was being told that qualitative research is 'proper' research – providing it's done properly of course. What goes on in schools is so complex and involves so many different perspectives that I think you often need a qualitative approach to begin to get some idea of what's going on.

(Student taking an MA in Sociology)

I really appreciate hearing about other researchers' experiences of doing research. It was quite a revelation when I first became aware that things don't always go as smoothly as some written accounts seem to suggest. It's really reassuring to hear honest reports: they alert you to pitfalls and problems and things that you might not have thought about.

(Doctoral student)

I am sure that comments such as these will be familiar to anyone who has ever taught or taken a course which aims to introduce the range of research approaches available to social scientists in general and those working in educational settings in particular.

The central message that they convey seems to be that the influence of the positivist scientist paradigm is both strong and pervasive, shaping expectations of what constitutes 'proper', 'valid' and 'worthwhile' research. What Barry Troyna wrote in 1994 continues to be the case; namely that:

> There is a view which is already entrenched and circulating widely in the populist circles . . . that qualitative research is subjective, value-laden and, therefore, unscientific and invalid, in contrast to quantitative research, which meets the criteria of being objective, value-free, scientific and therefore valid.
>
> (1994: 9)

Within academic and research circles though, where the development of postmodernist and post-structuralist ideas have affected both thinking and research practice, it can be easy to forget what the popular perspective is. This is because, in these communities, qualitative researchers from the range of theoretical standpoints utilize a variety of methods, approaches, strategies and techniques in the full confidence that their work is rigorous, legitimate and totally justifiable as research. And the process of peer review serves to confirm that confidence.

Recently, however, for those concerned with and involved in research in educational settings, and especially for those engaged in educational research, it seems that the positivist model, using experimental, scientific, quantitative methods, is definitely in the ascendancy once again. The signs are there to be read in, for example, the types of research that receive financial support, in the curricula that are being specified by funding councils for postgraduate research methods training programmes, and in the way in which those of us working in England and Wales entered the new millennium with the government-endorsed exhortation to produce evidence-based research that,

> (firstly) demonstrates conclusively that if teachers change their practice from x to y there will be significant and enduring improvement in teaching and learning; and (secondly) has developed an effective method of convincing teachers of the benefits of, and means to, changing from x to y.
>
> (Hargreaves, 1996: 5)

If it is to realize its commendable aims of school effectiveness and school improvement, research as portrayed here demands 'objectivity', experiments and statistical proofs. There is a problem with this requirement though, and the essence of it is that educational institutions and the individuals who are involved in and with them are a heterogeneous bunch with different attributes, abilities, aptitudes, aims, values, perspectives, needs and so on. Furthermore these institutions and individuals are located within complex social contexts with all the implications and influences that this entails. On its own, research whose findings can be expressed in mathematical terms is unlikely to be sophisticated enough to sufficiently accommodate and account for the myriad differences that are involved. As one group of prominent educational researchers have noted:

> We will argue that schooling does have its troubles. However, we maintain that the analysis of the nature and location of these troubles by the school effectiveness research literature, and in turn those writing Department for Employment and Education policy off the back of this research, is oversimplified, misleading and thereby educationally and politically dangerous (notwithstanding claims of honourable intent).
>
> (Slee et al. 1998: 2–3)

There is a need for rigorous research which does not ignore, but rather addresses, the complexity of the various aspects of schools and schooling; for research which explores and takes account of different objective experiences and subjective perspectives, and which acknowledges that qualitative information is essential, both in its own right and also in order to make full and proper use of quantitative indicators. The *Doing Qualitative Research in Educational Settings* series of books is based on this fundamental belief. Thus the overall aims of the series are: to illustrate the potential that particular qualitative approaches have for research in educational settings, and to consider some of the practicalities involved and issues that are raised when doing qualitative research, so that readers will feel equipped to embark on research of their own.

At this point it is worth noting that qualitative research is difficult to define as it means different things at different times and in different contexts. Having said this, Denzin and Lincoln's (2000) generic definition offers a useful starting point:

> Qualitative research is a situated activity that locates the observer in the world. It consists of a set of interpretive, material practices that make the world visible. These practices transform the world. They turn the world into a series of representations, including field notes, interviews, conversations, photographs, recordings and memos to the self. At this level, qualitative research involves an interpretive, naturalistic approach to the world. This means that qualitative researchers study things in their natural settings, attempting to make sense of, or interpret, phenomena in terms of the meanings people bring to them. Qualitative research involves the studied use and collection of a variety of empirical materials – case study; personal experience; introspection; life story; interview; artefacts; cultural texts and productions; observational, historical, interactional and visual texts – that describe routine and problematic moments and meanings in individuals' lives. Accordingly, qualitative researchers deploy a wide range of interconnected

methods, hoping always to get a better fix on the subject matter at hand. It is understood, however, that each practice makes the world visible in a different way. Hence there is frequently a commitment to using more than one interpretive practice in any study.

(Denzin and Lincoln 2000: 3–4)

All of the authors contributing to the series are established researchers with a wealth of experience on which to draw and all make use of specific and vivid examples from their own and others' work. A consequence of this use of examples is the way in which each writer conveys a sense of research being an intensely satisfying and enjoyable activity, in spite of the specific difficulties that are sometimes encountered.

Perhaps the chief difficulty that researchers who choose to use fictional approaches face is that of having their work accepted as a legitimate form of social enquiry. Convincing sceptical tutors and examiners of the value of stories is not easy, even though, as Laurel Richardson notes, throughout the twentieth century 'the relationship between social scientific writing and literary writing grew in complexity. The presumed solid demarcations between "fact" and "fiction" and between "true" and "imagined" were blurred' (2000: 926). Despite this blurring, not everyone would agree with Norman Denzin when he states that 'the narrative turn in the social sciences has been taken, we have told our stories from the field, and we understand today that we write culture' (2000: 898). There are still those who seek the Grail of objective and factual reporting of objective reality and who believe that language can be neutral.

In *Narratives and Fictions in Educational Research* Peter Clough attempts to demonstrate that truths about educational issues and concerns can be told through consciously and explicitly fictional devices. Furthermore, he suggests that fictional stories can make public those experiences and perceptions that other methodological approaches and research techniques are unable to reveal.

Narratives and Fictions in Educational Research differs from other books in the series in that Peter Clough wishes to let the stories he has composed speak for themselves. His view is that description, let alone prescription, of the creative process would be contradictory to the essence of the approach. Thus he provides a personal commentary or reading of each of his stories; readers seeking more specific detail must look elsewhere.

Narrative offers an exciting, important and, at this time, essentially exploratory way forward for educational research. Human beings are storying beings. It is natural for us to make sense of our lives, the lives of others and the contexts in which we live through telling and hearing/reading stories. *Narratives and Fictions in Educational Research* will give readers the confidence to try it for themselves.

Final note

It was Barry Troyna who initially came up with the idea for this series. Although his publishing career was extensive, Barry had never been a series editor and, in his inimitable way, was very keen to become one. Whilst he was probably best known for his work in the field of 'race', Barry was getting increasingly interested in issues to do with methodology when he became ill with the cancer which was eventually to kill him. It was during the twelve months of his illness that he and I drew up a proposal and approached potential authors. All of us knew that it was very likely that he would not live to see to see the series in print but he was adamant that it should go ahead, nonetheless. The series is, therefore, something of a memorial to him.

Pat Sikes

References

Denzin, N. and Lincoln, Y. (2000) Introduction: entering the field of qualitative research, in N. Denzin and Y. Lincoln (eds) *Handbook of Qualitative Research*, second edition. Thousand Oaks, CA: Sage.

Denzin, N. (2000) The practices and policies of interpretation, in N. Denzin and Y. Lincoln (eds) *Handbook of Qualitative Research*, second edition. Thousand Oaks, CA: Sage.

Hargreaves, D. (1996) Teaching as a research-based profession: possibilities and prospects. Teacher Training Agency Annual Lecture. London: TTA.

Richardson, L. (2000) Writing: a method of inquiry research, in N. Denzin and Y. Lincoln (eds) *Handbook of Qualitative Research*, second edition. Thousand Oaks, CA: Sage.

Slee, R. and Weiner, G. with Tomlinson, S. (eds) (1998) Introduction: school effectiveness for whom? in R. Slee, G. Weiner and S. Tomlinson *School Effectiveness for Whom? Challenges to the School Effectiveness and School Improvement Movements*. London: Falmer.

Troyna, B. (1994) Blind faith? Empowerment and educational research, *International Studies in the Sociology of Education*, 4(1): 3–24.

Acknowledgements

This text exists as a result of the opportunities afforded to me by many teachers, students, colleagues and friends. Some know the support and inspiration I have derived from the many interactions in seminars, teaching sessions and discussion. I want to record my sincere thanks for the questions, challenges and suggestions which have arisen from these exchanges.

There are some people I should like to acknowledge by name as this text owes much to their involvement. I should like to thank:

Wilfred Carr, for his comments on parts of the text and his ongoing support for my writing; Felicity Armstrong, Annie Bee, Tim Booth, David Bridges, Barbara Cole, Danny Goodley, Mo Griffiths, Michelle Moore, Jon Nixon, Cathy Nutbrown, Jenny Ozga, Andy Sparkes, Bill Tierney, Claire Tregaskis, Melanie Walker and Jack Whitehead for their critical enthusiasm; my teachers Neil Bolton, Stuart Manger, Albert Metcalfe and Brenda Thomas for their faith and example; Shona Mullen, of Open University Press, for her encouragement, insight and enthusiasm for the text; the editors and anonymous referees of a number of journals including *Qualitative Inquiry, Qualitative Studies in Education, Narrative Inquiry, Auto/Biography*.

The story of *Klaus* is reprinted by kind permission of Taylor and Francis. The story of *Molly* is reprinted by kind permission of Sage Publications. The story of *Rob* is reprinted by kind permission of Sage Publications Inc. The story of *Bev* is reprinted by kind permission of *Auto/Biography* (British Sociological Association). The story of *Lolly* is reprinted by kind permission of Taylor and Francis. The extract from *The Man with the Blue Guitar* by Wallace Stevens is reproduced with kind permission from Faber and Faber.

Peter Clough
Sheffield

The blue guitar
Becomes the place of things as they are,
A composing of senses of the guitar.
Wallace Stevens

Preface: The Man with the Blue Guitar

The man bent over his guitar,

writes the poet Wallace Stevens (1965: 52)*,

A shearsman of sorts. The day was green.

They said, 'You have a blue guitar,
You do not play things as they are.'

The man replied, 'Things as they are
Are changed upon the blue guitar.'

And they said then, 'But play, you must,
A tune beyond us, yet ourselves,

A tune upon the blue guitar
Of things exactly as they are.'

And so begins Stevens's long, curious essay on art. The guitarist continues:

I cannot bring a world quite round,
Although I patch it as I can.

I sing a hero's head, large eye
And bearded bronze, but not a man,

Although I patch him as I can
And reach through him almost to man.

---

* From *The Collected Poems of Wallace Stevens* by Wallace Stevens, copyright 1954 by Wallace Stevens and renewed 1982 by Holly Stevens. Used by permission of Alfred A. Knopf, a division of Random House, Inc.

. . .

Ah, but to play man number one,
To drive the dagger in his heart,

To lay his brain upon the board
And pick the acrid colours out,

To nail his thoughts across the door . . .

. . .

A million people on one string?
And all their manner in the thing,

And all their manner, right and wrong,
And all their manner, weak and strong?

Stevens's subject is ostensibly art, and its ability to represent things to us. In its complete, 27 pages the poem is also effectively an essay in epistemology and ontology, though clearly its form has little or nothing to do with propositional argument. In fact, the greatest achievement of the poem is to dissolve any separate notions of content and form so that 'poetry is the subject of the poem'.

To be sure, the guitarist and his words can point to things, can 'sing a hero's head, large eye/And bearded bronze', but these creations are 'not a man/Although I patch him as I can/And reach through him almost to man'. These are artefacts which are, of course, not 'the thing itself'. But for Stevens, art does not even *refer* to 'the thing itself'; it may (as John Berger said of photography) '*quote* from reality'(Berger 1996: 23, emphasis added) but its ultimate effect stands free of the object, the artist and the audience – though it must reach into all three. And for Stevens, it is the guitar which assembles for one moment 'A tune beyond us, yet ourselves . . . /Of things exactly as they are'.

Doesn't this sound like the 'crisis of representation' in social science (Denzin 1997) writ large as art? For Stevens's guitarist knows he cannot 'play man number one', and 'nail his thoughts across the door'; nor can he capture 'A million people on one string/And all their manner in the thing'. And, just so, social science inquiry has become self-consciously uneasy with its claims to speak of either unique or general human experience. Above all, perhaps, we are sceptical in postmodernity of the instruments which mediate researcher and researched.

I have adopted Wallace Stevens's poem for my purposes because he has written *at once* a thesis *on* art and a work *of* art. His methodology is thus embodied in the text itself, and this is what I have tried to do in the stories which form the central part of the book: to blur distinctions not only between form and content, but also between researcher and researched, between data and imagination; to insist, that is, that language itself, by itself, does the work of inquiry, without recourse to the meta-languages of methodology.

1 | Stories from educational settings: an introduction

> if data are the foundation on which knowledge rests, [then] it is
> important to trouble the common-sense understanding of that signifier, in
> postfoundational research that aims to produce different knowledge, and
> to produce knowledge differently.
>
> (St Pierre 1997: 176)

This is without doubt an uneven – and, in Marcus's (1994) sense, *messy* –
text, but it is not without scheme! It differs from the general scope and
schemes of the other books in the series quite deliberately, because it is primarily an attempt to 'trouble the common-sense understanding' of data; to
'produce different knowledge, and to produce knowledge differently'. It
is not so much a 'how to do' as a 'what is it possible to do?' text. This is
because my storying methodology in educational settings is an emerging
field: exciting and important, but still largely exploratory. And this is just
one way of carrying out research under postmodern conditions. My own
methods are thus presented simply as exemplars of an infinite number of
ways of reconceiving approaches to research reports.

I do not wish to make any claims about the quality of the stories which
are at the centre of this book; this is for the reader to decide. But I do want
to claim that I have successfully laid bare some of the ways in which meaning is created and communicated in research processes. In a period of the
'crisis of representation' (Denzin 1997) the work thus helps redefine the
relations of subject with object, of researcher and researched identities, and
of knowing with the known.

My intention in putting the book together in this particular form is to
make available to other students and researchers some modest, though con-
crete, examples of experiments in making data. Other texts – including those
in this series – may offer panoptic and critical accounts of method and
methodology; in the course of doing this, some will locate their arguments
in relation to postmodern inquiry. But it seems to me that postmodern

research in educational settings needs at this time not so much to be talked about critically and retrospectively, as to be exemplified. Though postmodern inquiry is often described by commentators, it is surely given with its nature that it cannot be prescribed. So the task becomes less one of counting up quotations than of determining for oneself the meaning, process and significance of postmodern inquiry. This book, then, is one such – inevitably personal – account.

This will perhaps give a confidence of sorts to those – particularly research students – who wish to experiment in their designs, but who feel constrained by the received traditions of practice and examination. (For this reason I have included an attempt at rational justification – in this case of fictional approaches – which I think will stand up fairly well to rigorous academic critique; it may at the least provide a few timbers for others' methodologies!) My greatest hope is that readers will see beyond the particular locality of my own work with stories to the larger and more general issues of representation which currently occupy social science inquiry.

Specifically, I hope that readers will feel encouraged and enabled to develop inquiries which not only throw light on their objects, but also simultaneously transform the means by which they do this. (For this purpose I make frequent reference in the book to the case of art, where form and content will never easily be separated.) And I take for granted that, in any field of inquiry, research of human significance is by definition always straining at the limits of its method, ultimately troubled in its methodology.

For all these reasons, my book departs from the usual series format which provides guidance in developing particular methods. This is not to trivialize those methods, or to minimize the vital need to study and understand them; indeed, they are the tools we almost involuntarily reach for when our curiosity is stirred. But the view developed throughout the book is that methods are uniquely created in the presence and service of quite particular contexts of moral and political need. These contexts are often three-dimensional, but they are also constructions of our own selves, the ultimate sources of data.

The structure of the book

In common with the other books in the series I offer some historical context to the approach under discussion, I discuss epistemological issues, and I show some of the processes that are entailed in my work. However, this book differs from those others in terms of the sequence in which those discussions take place. You will not find, for example, a section headed 'Historical background to fictional methodology', because I present the book as a self-consciously postmodern text, designed as an exemplar of the writing of its 'moment' (Lincoln 1995). Rather, such discussion is embedded in the text at points when such histories are useful.

Throughout the book I have placed 'hints', rather than prescriptions, about how to approach storying methodology, but it would be a contradiction of the book's epistemology to include a section which says 'How to write a story', for how *I* write a story will not be a matter of *method* as such, but of personal, moral and ethical response to research experiences. Throughout the book you will find a perpetual concern with ethics and moral positioning in relation to derivation of data, ownership of data, issues of honesty and integrity. Essentially though, it is not so much what *I* think about these issues which is important, but how you respond to these prompts which really matters. For it is your own ethical and moral position which will inform your research designs. What I am offering here is not a model to be followed but an example to be reflected upon. You will see, too, how I have approached the tasks of (to use the traditional terms) 'data analysis' and 'presentation of findings'. These research acts happen, but in postmodern methodology they are not easily separated into distinct analytical stages.

So why is this book so different from its partners in this series of *Doing Qualitative Research in Educational Settings*? It is different because the whole book radically questions much of the taken-for-granted purposes, processes and effects of inquiry. Central to my exemplification of narrative methodology are five differently constructed stories. They must speak for themselves. So, as the stories are central to the rest of the text, the critical discussion must fit 'around' the stories. And it is certain that 'stories' do not conform to the 'step-by-step guide' that you might expect to find in a discussion of a particular methodological approach.

The book, resting on Wallace Stevens's poem, *The Blue Guitar*, begins with an opening chapter which sets out some background and gives my justification for using stories as a means of research creation and report. The heart of the book comes next, in the form of five stories (Chapters 3–7). They have this order because they portray mounting difficulty both in the content and in the experimentation with 'form'. Chapter 8 follows the stories and provides my 'readings' of those stories, followed by Chapter 9, which locates the meaning and value of stories in educational settings to educational research generally. Finally, in Chapter 10, I explore the legitimation of fictional writing in educational and social science inquiry.

How to read this book

Having explained the organization of the text and said that this book is different, I should make some suggestions as to how to read it. I think the book offers logical progression through the chapters; I have presented it here in this way because *I* think this is the best way to read it. I would thus suggest first reading my account of narrative in educational inquiry, then go on to read the five stories (as examples of that methodology), and finally to attend to the various discussions which follow. You may prefer, however, to read Chapter 8 before you read the stories, so that you read the stories knowing what *I* had in mind (though I think that what *you* have in mind *as you read the stories* is the more important moment of meaning). Perhaps the best way to read this book is to let the stories speak to you first (without the interruption of my own methodological and ethical positioning) and then to move on to my own readings of them. Some may prefer to contemplate Chapters 9 and 10 *before* reading the stories – they provide some grounding for the stories and thus answer some of the questions which the stories and the readings raise. However you choose to organize your reading, there will be an inevitable 'back and forth' between stories and readings, experience and analysis. Throughout the book you will find exemplification of the crises of representation within the context of educational research in general and educational settings specifically.

Writing stories from educational settings

How do we write stories from educational settings?

> Although we are freer to present our texts in a variety of forms to diverse audiences, we have different constraints arising from self-consciousness about claims to authorship, authority, truth, validity, and reliability. Self-reflexivity unmasks complex political/ideological agendas hidden in our writing. Truth claims are less easily validated now; desires to speak 'for' others are suspect. The greater freedom to experiment with textual form, however, does not guarantee a better product. The opportunities for writing worthy texts – books and articles that are a 'good read' – are multiple, exciting and demanding. But the work is harder. The guarantees are fewer. There is a lot more for us to think about.
>
> (Richardson 1994: 523)

This book is *primarily* about possible responses to the 'crisis of representation', and its concern with fictional writing as social science inquiry is therefore a later and contingent function of that. Given this, the book offers guidance on writing stories through its exposition of some of the thinking processes that have gone on in my own attempts to 'trouble the common-sense understanding of [data] in postfoundational research that aims to produce different knowledge, and to produce knowledge differently' (St Pierre 1997: 176). My hope is that by seeing something of my own radical structures of inquiry, readers will be encouraged and enabled to make their own attempts to redefine research.

One of the difficulties that I struggle with in representing my own stories as methodologically legitimate for social science inquiry is how to teach the methods entailed. How should I tell a research student, say, or an interested colleague how to set about making persuasive stories? What is the canon, where the instructive exemplars, what the criteria for falsifiability? This is not to say that there are no criteria and no rules; there are – as Richardson (1994) asserts – multiple and complex criteria, but it is not possible in the postmodern turn to offer prescription. But the notion that, freed from the restrictive and prescriptive structures in the tradition of academic writing, we can construct our own narrative report in a style of our choosing (and thus with some ease) is a mischief. For while is it possible to state with some clarity how to structure research report which presents, say, the findings of an experimental study, the narrative form does not render itself so easily to the application of such formulae.

If we think of the writing of stories in educational research as the creation of a building, the writer becomes architect. The question, therefore, is not technical; it is not '*how* do I *construct* this building?' but rather 'what is this building *for*?' Questions of purpose and function follow – 'what must it *do*?', 'who is it *for*?' So, in setting out to write a story, the primary work is in the interaction of ideas; in the act of thinking, tuning in, decision making and focusing on the primary intent of the work. And of course, writing a story – like constructing a building – is not carried out outside of a need, a community, a context. These are actually the primary ingredients.

As you will see in the five stories in this book, they employ different tools to do their work, and these tools are developed from the personal study of *form*. In my own writing I make a point of seeking out the novelists who are perfecting their own form – Winterson, Didion, Crace, among others – and I look at the devices they use to convey their message. I ask not only 'What is this about?', but also 'How did they make that work?' So, as Richardson (1994: 523) reminds us – 'the work is harder. The guarantees are fewer. There is a lot more for us to think about.'

Why is the story approach useful in educational research?

Narrative is useful only to the extent that it opens up (to its audiences) a deeper view of life in familiar contexts: it can make the familiar strange, and the strange familiar. As a means of educational report, stories can provide a means by which those truths, which cannot be otherwise told, are uncovered. The fictionalization of educational experience offers researchers the opportunity to import fragments of data from various real events in order to speak to the heart of social consciousness – thus providing the protection of anonymity to the research participants without stripping away the rawness of real happenings. I have tried to do this in all five of the stories included in this volume; they are stories which *could* be true, they derive from real events and feelings and conversations, but they *are* ultimately fictions: versions of the truth which are woven from an amalgam of raw data, real details and (where necessary) *symbolic equivalents* (Yalom 1991). Stories are further important to research in educational settings because they allow the report of those experiences which might otherwise not be made public by other 'traditional' tools of the trade.

I am not arguing that all research should be reported through fictionalized narrative, but that *some* researchers might develop the capacity to make art if they are fully to embrace the postmodern ethnographic project in the twenty-first century. The idea of methodological regulation, then, is importantly shifted from material to moral accountability, and, to echo Richardson (1994: 523) thus: 'Self-reflexivity [within the written story] unmasks complex political/ideological agendas'. Those agenda are alerted throughout the book, in the stories themselves and in Chapters 8 and 9. As you read, you will – I hope – develop from my argument your own rationale for the importance of story in educational research.

Life story, life history and stories from educational settings

Although I have not chosen to explore this in detail in the book, there are some important connections to be made between my stories and the cognate practices of life stories and life-history study. (For a full account of the latter, see Goodson and Sikes 2001.) I have not, however, been content to take a life story and analyse it to produce a life history using the sorts of tools that are normally provided and which hence separate subject and methods, form and content (see Tierney 1995). But I have drawn on the *events* of lived experience to create fictional stories of lives lived.

An important point about the construction of such stories (and their dis/connection with life-historical research) is that they do not depend exclusively on any one form of data; they might as likely come from a 'troubling' of survey as much as of interview data; of documentary as much as of observational evidence. Interestingly, although I was led – to some extent – to the stories through an attraction to life-history work, and have continued tacitly to assume something cognate in the approaches, I now realize that to try to relate my stories to such work directly would have no specific relevance. As textual *jouissance* (Barthes 1975), such stories can be derived from *any* data: the important moment of creation is synthetic (and thus draws purposively and fitfully on data as well as dreams, hunches and histories, causes and cases, transcriptions and transgressions, morals and meanings). So, I am telling *my* versions of stories which I have created as a result of *my own* interactions and intuitions, remembering Richardson's warning that . . . 'desires to speak "for" others are suspect' (1994: 523).

Narrative and academic traditions

As the communication of knowledge in the social sciences is realized in large measure through language, so the task of the researcher is so to dispose words that they tell a story – in its very simplest sense – about the phenomena from which they draw their meaning. This notion of story holds equally for a statistical analysis and a rich ethnography: both accounts respect the unities of time and place which are essential to narrative meaning.

In the final chapter of this book (Chapter 10) I have drawn heavily on phenomenological philosophy as an ultimate justification for the method of inquiry which my stories represent. Some – perhaps many – readers will not find this *ultimately* persuasive at all. It is compelling for me, however, because of a *faith* I hold in phenomenology which cannot be explained by a 'mere' logic. My own phenomenology is not merely academic, but rather issues from Husserl's (1970: 221) view that 'it is called upon to bring about a complete personal transformation which might be compared to religious conversion'. I make this point here because my own attempts at research in the postmodern turn are wholly expressions of my own 'moral career', and the *beliefs* I have come to hold about the nature of consciousness. These are my ways of seeing the world I both create and inhabit.

Merleau-Ponty (1962: xiii, original emphasis) says of the study of phenomenology that it is 'less a question of counting up quotations than of discovering this *phenomenology for ourselves*', and I suggest that this is similarly my book's chief didactic point: that its readers learn not how to write stories as such, but rather something of the much more radical architecture of making and communicating data *for their own moral and political purposes.*

This is difficult work, and as you will see in the stories which follow, the freedom from imposed structural frameworks of academic tradition does not mean freedom from every dilemma. As Richardson reminds us:

> Although we are freer to present our texts in a variety of forms to diverse audiences, we have different constraints arising from self-consciousness about claims to authorship, authority, truth, validity, and reliability.
>
> (Richardson 1994: 523)

2 | The map is not the terrain . . .

Je ne cherche pas, je trouve.[1]

(Picasso 1923: 11)

Everyone, at some time in their life, must choose whether to stay with a ready-made world that may be safe but which is also limiting, or to push forward, often past the frontiers of common-sense, into a personal place, unknown and untried. In *Oranges are Not the Only Fruit* this quest is one of sexuality as well as individuality. Superficially, it seems specific . . . in fact, *Oranges* deals absolutely with emotions and confrontations that none of us can avoid. First love, loss, grief, rage and above all courage, these are the engines that drive the narrative through the peculiar confines of the story . . . Is *Oranges* an autobiographical novel? No not at all and yes of course.

(Winterson 1991: xiv)

This chapter provides a basis for understanding terms, terminologies and practices as understood in ethnographic studies and narrative reporting, and locates 'story' in terms of current critical debate, the development of narrative methodologies, and the identity of the researcher within the ethnographic project. As a research text, this book is concerned with the continuities of literary and ethnographic approaches to human experience, and specifically with how inquiries using fictional forms may be realized in social science studies. To achieve this I have placed the major emphasis on demonstration. I draw on some critical argument, but devote the central part of the book to a collection of stories which, while derived from data, are ostensibly 'fictional'. As such, they must speak for themselves. I realize that I must, however, speak on their behalf to a critically conscious research audience, and so in each case I have assembled some fuzzy maps which show something of how the stories were found, and how those processes might be explained within the furniture of a methodological critique. All of this I take to be expressive of the 'crisis of representation' (Denzin 1997).

Recent years have seen significant methodological developments in the ethnographic study of schools and other social institutions, and perhaps particularly in the development of auto/biographical (see, for examples, Erben 1998; Rosen 2000) or otherwise life-historical methods (see, for examples, Hatch and Wisniewski 1998; Goodson and Sikes 2001). Broadly, such inquiry seeks to relate the 'micro' world of the individual to the 'macro' world of institutional meanings which they both inhabit and re-create. At its most fundamental, this is inquiry into the relations between subject and object.

Of course, the question of subject–object relations occupies all methodological discussion, but is distinctively characteristic of recent critique in ethnography, where the 'crisis of representation' (Denzin 1997) reveals the confusion of writer, text and subject matter. Typical questions asked include: What does a given text 'represent'? Is it the 'subject's' experience? Is it the 'author's'? Or, reflexively, is it the 'reader's'? And – in any case – how is it to be 'validated'? Responses to these regressive questions reach into varying epistemologies, and their forms of 'report' are realized in 'new' or 'alternative' media, as for example, 'messy text' (Marcus 1994), 'performance text' (Denzin 1997), 'performance science' (Becker et al. 1989) or 'Readers' Theatre' (Bacon 1979). My own (very messy) text, based on stories found and made in schools, adds a voice to these discussions.

So the book does three things; it

- *locates* stories from educational settings within the traditions of social/educational research and the 'crises of representation'
- *exemplifies* such stories
- *discovers* some of the processes of composition, and so questions assumptions about the distinctness of researcher and researched, and about the very nature of social science data.

To achieve these aims, I have tried to go beyond the typical justifications for narrative research which are drawn from social science methodologies, and to borrow from the methodologies of literary composition. Although Denzin (1997) suggests some limited convergence of debate, the common ground of the literary and the ethnographic project has yet to be significantly explored, and in this book I have tried to address this relationship. As I have said, this is not, however, a methodology text in any traditional sense. Although set about with some critical discussion, it is an important function of my thesis that the stories which are at the heart of the text carry with them implicitly their own methodological terms (for a related discussion of this, see also Crotty 1998: ch. 5).

Methods and maps

Several writers (Sandelowski 1994; Tierney 1995, 1998; Rosen 2000) have begun to mark out the ground on which a more evidently aesthetic research form – specifically through the use of story*telling* – can be constructed. A broad thesis at work in these accounts is that there is a characteristically narrative structure to consciousness, that we are always making sense of our lives in stories of one form or another; thus – it might be argued – even the quantitatively based research report has a story to tell because such research inevitably involves human experience even though the research design might seek to exclude such. MacIntyre's (1985) expression of the 'unity of a human life' develops this theme: we think in stories, and every researcher asks, consciously or otherwise, 'What is the story I wish to tell?' We can be sure only that there are other stories beneath every published refereed research report, though many of those stories are likely never to be told.

The crisis of apology

This text takes off from Norman Denzin's (1997) *Interpretive Ethnography: Ethnographic Practices for the 21st Century*. Denzin provides a history and a prospectus for ethnography which is panoptic and bold; a reading of Denzin's geography of the ethnographic project will help the reader to locate my own fictional texts in terms of the epistemologies which Denzin sees attached (or inchoate) in current realizations of ethnographic inquiry.

I would not presume to tell readers what to look for in Denzin's *Interpretive Ethnography*, for they will find in it according to what they bring to it. What I can do is provide a brief 'review' of the scope of the text, and my own indication of importance of this text *for me*. Denzin's publishers describe the work thus:

> As the world's culture has become both postmodern and multinational, so too must ethnography. In this volume, Norman K. Denzin examines the changes and sounds a call to transform ethnographic writing in a manner befitting a new age.
>
> The author ponders the prospects, problems and forms of ethnographic interpretive writing in the twenty-first century. He argues cogently and persuasively that postmodern ethnography is the moral discourse of the contemporary world, and that ethnographers can and should explore new types of experimental texts – performance based texts, literary journalism and narratives of the self – to form a new ethics of inquiry.
>
> (www.sagepub.co.uk)

Interpretive Ethnography is then presented in three parts:

- *Reading the crisis* systematically alerts the crises of 'representation, legitimation and praxis' which are said to confront 'qualitative researchers in the human disciplines';
- *Experiential texts* discusses the emergence of texts which emphasize vision and insight, and emphasizes the crucial role of lived experience;
- *Whose truth?* exposes the writing and reading of narrative from two positions – that of the 'old' form where narrative is not for experiment or criticism, and the 'sixth moment' where narrative form can be freshly manipulated by ethnographers to create new truths.

I find in Denzin an exciting text which demands new form and new responsibilities for ethnographic report. What is missing in Denzin's text, however, is *demonstration*. That is why I have organized my text as it is – glancing off many of Denzin's standpoints, but placing the emphasis first (and essentially) on *demonstration* and (only) second on *argument*. As I have discussed elsewhere in this text, much has been written about the importance of narrative, yet there remain pitifully few examples of stories which report lived experience in educational settings.

This is to say that I neither uncritically accept the whole of Denzin's thesis, nor that I am letting Denzin do the prolegomenary work which I should myself do. Rather, I wish to get urgently to the texts which I have written – I want *them* to do the talking – and to do so with a minimum of methodological apologia. Thus this text stands against a background provided by Denzin. Must you read Denzin before reading on? That depends on what you hope to gain from this book. My urgency is demonstration – the stories themselves – but in so far as we need platforms upon which to build and interpretive devices through which to make meaning, then Denzin is an important part of the structure!

This is, of course, a particular methodological position in itself. It arises as a function of the 'crisis of representation' (see, particularly, Denzin 1997: 3–5) and may be called the *crisis of apology*. At its simplest, such a crisis describes the paradoxes which a writer of interpretive ethnography faces in explicitly, *critically* locating a text for an audience. Of course, for many other, more traditional research processes this is not a problem; indeed, a defining characteristic – a sine qua non – of research is that it makes explicit the traditions of inquiry and terms of procedure which give it significance and validity. There *is* a problem, however, where the text depends – on pain of ceasing to be – on devices of construction and representation which *will not* be made explicit; texts where the terms on which meaning is constructed are not made patent as formal indices of validity, but are seamlessly identical with the subject as constituted by the literary form itself. In these cases method/ology is not a discrete frame or lens which seeks to justify an essentially separate, ensuing report with reference to devices of *validation*; it is rather embedded in the voices of the text which by themselves seek *verification* persuasively in the lived world of the reader.

In the visual arts (see Prosser 1998) by contrast, form and content are more obviously inseparable: the strength of the subject is wholly continuous with the form through which it is communicated. Should we expect any less of a research which is essentially about human experience? The separation of 'data' and 'analysis' troubles me, and it seems to me that in life-history work it is almost a contradiction in terms to 'give' a life history and then analyse it when it should be seamlessly self-analytical. For that reason the stories from research in this book stand on their own. The work of criticism then becomes not one of a social science but rather a literary criticism in which one might characteristically talk about character, plot and so on; and one might talk as the literary critic does about how and when and under what circumstances a particular literary work was composed.

Booth (1996) has argued the peculiar power which narrative methods may have for bringing to life the experience of people traditionally conceived of as 'inarticulate'; such an approach, based in empirical data, already has something of a long tradition. However, what is more radical about Booth's argument is a plea for the admission of the fictional construction of experience as a research form no less legitimate – and considerably more persuasive – than any other. Acknowledging that the elaboration of criteria for evaluating such a project have yet to be worked out, Booth says:

> Standard tests such as reliability, validity and replicability are neither appropriate nor adequate when lives are not consistent, biographical truth is a will-o'-the-wisp and stories *inevitably reflect something of the teller*. Narratives may be better judged by aesthetic standards, by their emotive force or their capacity to engage the reader emotionally in the story being told, by their verisimilitude rather than their verifiability and by criteria of authenticity or integrity concerned with how far stories are true to the lives of those they portray.
>
> (Booth 1996: 37, added emphasis)

The fictional narratives that Booth is talking of are importantly – or apparently – 'about' others. There are few examples of the form used to convey the experience of *both* the subject *and* the researcher, though it is something of a truism that stories are *always* about their authors, for in any writing 'we are never more (and sometimes less) than the co-authors of our own narratives' (MacIntyre 1985: 213).

The exemplary case for narrative as a means of reporting experience *in and of* itself is that of works of literature. My tongue was not wholly in cheek when I first noticed this in justification of my submission to a social science journal of a text largely without explicit methodological apparatus. My text – the text which I wanted to draw attention to – was a story which

I had crafted from 'data', but more importantly from the hunches and insights which probably lay behind my attraction to those phenomena in the first place. I footnoted my concern with

> [the] dilemma given with the challenge to write social science as art. I sometimes rehearse it to myself thus: when William Shakespeare presented *Romeo and Juliet*, he did *not* preface the work with something like: 'In the context of erotic, inter- and intra-familial psycho- and socio-dynamic struggle, this dramatised ethnographic study examines the lives of an adolescent male and a female subject who . . .'; nor, for that matter, did *Dallas* carry a methodological *apologia*. These works come without such announcement because they seek verification only as story; long before the critics come to them, they all contain the bulk of the terms on which they shall be read within the texts themselves.
>
> (Clough 1999: 429)

Can ethnography do the same, and still *be* ethnography?

Language and identity

In the stories which follow, there is a particular account of language at work (explored in more detail in Chapter 10). Briefly, language is not to be seen as being 'about', as 'referring to', but as creative of objects. Language does not describe – for example – characters to the point where they are 'pinned down' but rather language glances *off* objects just as it 'glances off' experience. I think that my own discovery of this character of language started when I tried to write a story about Nick (I have never 'finished' or published the story though I draw on the experience of writing it many times). The central problem in writing this story was the experience I had of trying to characterize a particular teacher – Nick – his school, and the extreme difficulties which both were experiencing, and I drew on Williams's (1969) idea of the mutually constructive relation of organism and organization. However, in the end my account is achieved not by 'faithfully' reporting the 'facts', but on the contrary by giving in to an invasive image I had of Nick which certainly did not come from the interview 'data'. When I came to write of Nick there was no method within the means of research which would allow me to evoke him for a reader without violating, through reduction, the nervous complex of meanings which meeting and working with him provoked. Earlier characters I had rendered this way, slipping the pieces of their lives easily into boxes labelled with the cyphers and stuff of a social science. However, Nick would not go in. Nick would not 'go in' because I knew the original 'Nick' very very well, I had spent many hours sharing cigarettes, experiences, fears, joys.

More importantly, I had thought to uncover Nick, and all the others, without realizing the absurdity of my own position; here I was presuming to tease apart the threads which made up the cultural patterns of personal and institutional life without so much as a glance at those which organized my own way of seeing; and without which those other lives would be invisible to me. But I *could* put what I knew and felt of him into certain stories which would themselves carry the analysis:

> After three days of looking for Nick [in the transcriptions] I found him in my imagination. What I wrote was made in my own store of 'knowledge' and, free of the 'facts', seemed to say more of Nick and Nick in school than ever he had said or could have said. [For] in excitedly attaching the organism/organization idea, and eagerly attaching badges to analyse that relationship, I had forgotten my own insertion in this particular culture: the organism that was/is me and which would inevitably mediate whatever I saw and felt. And my 'understanding of others' – in this case Nick and his school – came not from the data spilling from the tea-chests, nor from any reading of the literature but, indeed, from a setting aside of those things; and from a simple act of imagination that could only have sprung from my own experience. It doesn't matter whether what I wrote about Nick took place in fact; it takes place in an act of imagination driven by profound symbols; the event symbolises in a way which data and analysis could never do.
>
> (Clough 1995: 134)

My struggle to portray Nick as he was *to me* began my project – since that time – to explore ways of researching/writing which could do a rich justice at the same time to my 'subjects' as to myself as the organizing consciousness. For, despite the sterility of instruments, we never come innocent to a research task, or a situation of events; rather we situate these events not merely in the institutional meanings which our profession provides, but also constitute them as expressions of ourselves. This is – at one level – mainly to acknowledge positionality. More importantly though, it is also a statement about the essentially distinctive and creative organization of all research.

My concern in this book is to bring together the literary exploration of life and self through fiction with some of the furniture of the ethnographic project, and so to question whether and how the two projects draw on different *versions of truth*.

Of his paintings Picasso famously said: 'the artist must know the manner whereby to convince others of the truthfulness of his lies' (1923: 7). This is what I am seeking to do with the stories in this section, to use literary techniques and the sources of research data to create the truths of professional and personal lives. Thus the purpose of the book is identical with the central backbone of any art/istic endeavour, which is to tell the truth as one sees it. Therefore data may have to be manipulated to serve that larger purpose.

That is to say that the 'real' events may well undergo transformation, at the researcher's will, in order to tell a (particular) story – a *version* of the truth as the researcher sees it.

Stories of 'truths': senses composed

> When you talk with me about my research, do not ask me what I found; 1 found nothing. Ask me what I invented, what I made up from and out of my data. But know that in asking you to ask me this, I am not confessing to telling any lies about the people or events in my studies/stories. I have told the truth. The proof is in the things I have made – how they look to your mind's eye, whether they satisfy your sense of style and craftsmanship, whether you believe them, and whether they appeal to your heart.
>
> (Sandelowski 1994: 121)

Each of the next five chapters is, in effect, a free-standing short story with its own account of human and educational difficulty. The five stories each draw variously on different forms of narrative style. The presentation of the stories in this book offer a sense of mounting difficulty, both in their ostensible topics and in what they demand of the reader. The stories require investment – of energy and emotion and intellect – and so will speak differently to different people. But a common feature of the stories is that they all revolve around difficulty and sometimes tragedy. They are about suffering, misfortune and injustice and have a capacity to shock, to affront. The stories of Klaus, Rob, Molly and Bev, for example, are not stories that would normally be told in the usual run of research reporting, and although researchers are rightly held responsible for their publications, few are called to account in the manner portrayed in *Lolly: the Final Word*.

Though there are a number of ethnographic studies of the issues which, for example, are raised in *Molly*, here the task of that story is to appeal, in Sandelowski's phrase, in some way to your heart. (Of course, the heart is a funny thing, none less so than that of the social scientist, who by definition mediates its beat professionally with rhythms drawn from their discipline, and – to stretch the metaphor – skipping a beat now and then.)

Finally, while the stories in this book are to be read apart from critical apparatus as stories which speak for and of themselves, I have assembled, in Chapter 8, a series of 'readings' of each of the stories. In each of these readings I offer a different encounter with each story, where I bring together both the sources and contexts which prompted and nourished the stories, and sketch what I find in each of them. The readings present a means of exploring both the empirical contexts of the stories, and aspects of methodology which are problematized by them. Though inevitably compromised, this structure enables me to create a suitably temporary, postmodern *and yet self-consciously* hybrid text (Richardson 1994).

Note

1 'I do not seek, I find.'

3 | Klaus

I've met my father and his sons in so many special schools.

A man I was really frightened of was a miner from Bresswell; he had served in the post-war army, mainly in Germany, and named his son Klaus in honour and memory, I presume, of a greater life, culture and identity than he enjoyed in this bleak mining village. He had a bayonet over the fireplace. His wife – the mother – had left years before and he had brought Klaus up largely alone with some help from his nearby mother. He was in all respects what would be called, I think, 'a man's man'.

He was 5 foot 8 or so, but broad, and naturally fatty, but strong, too. His face was clearly made to be young – you could see him easily at 20, a sort of Irish look – but had been badly spoiled with hard work, drink and tobacco. It was a face long closed down; the man was only 35 or so, but the face had long since done with growing, and its chubbiness was made by the deep, finished lines of a man twice his age. His eyes were little points of dead carbon.

Klaus had the face of an angel, he really did; he had one of those scrubbed, beamish faces that children wear in photographs of working-class life in the 1950s, his dark hair parted minutely at the side and brylcreamed flat. But his eyes: his eyes were just simple agates of cornflowers, deep and waxy, and quite without resolution. You couldn't ever look into these eyes and read this or that; there was no trespass beyond them, what happened behind them was utterly private. The father gave Klaus his chin, his cheeks and his clothes, his swagger – in fact, almost everything. Once you'd seen the father, you could not see Klaus without the sight – the feeling – was organized by the man. God knows where those eyes came from, maybe they were his mother's, but in any event they must many times have driven that brutal man wild that he couldn't poke or prise or bludgeon a way behind them.

I know without 'evidence' that he was brutal; anyone could see the perfect shape of terror under the tissue of Klaus's rude confidence. I know he was brutal because he made me feel just like my father did: everything I said sounded hollow in his presence. Klaus was 8 and you could have written his future after only 10 minutes with him. Later that year he strangled the school's greylag goose.

My job was to liaise between home and the special school which Klaus attended in respect of his maladjustment. I made my first visit to the house during the half-term holiday in February. Bresswell is low, somehow; there is a severe grid of council estate painted on top of the slight wold of the East Midlands. The miners and their families live over the shop: quite beneath the estate is their work, so these are single-storey bungalows laid out as Coniston Drive, Langdale Close, Bowness Avenue and so on.

I had written – twice – that I was coming, but there was no sign of life when I arrived at 11. The curtains were drawn at all the windows and this was the only bungalow where there was no smoke from the chimney though this was a February morning. I knocked and banged and I would have gone just as the door opened.

'Now then, what the fuck . . .'

'It's me. It's Mr Clough. Mr Clough from the school.'

He was trying hard to focus on me; something stirred in him, but he was very drunk – still – and he had woken up too quickly. He was rubbing fiercely at his eyes, kneading the lids down so they creaked and they flashed red meat; and his blue chin rasped as his palms followed the work of his fingers. He was wearing a vest and brown trousers which he had spoiled somehow; there was a wet circle around his groin and then wet across one hip and down to the knee.

I can see myself standing there in my blue Harris Tweed jacket and saying 'It's Mr Clough. Mr Clough from the school.' Try it: there are not many ways to say those words and even fewer meanings.

He smelled of spent drink and the smell of the dark house reached out from behind him. Behind him I could see Klaus asleep on his back on a settee, open-mouthed and open-limbed.

'Shall I give you time to get up, you're obviously [obviously for God's sake] . . . I could come back in an hour?'

Actually, he hadn't heard a thing. He was working hard to get his eyes to hold me. When he spoke it was with immense effort: an impulse voiced with barely a movement of his lips though the string of sense was clear.

'Who the fuck is he? Who are you? What do you want?'

And I said again and louder: 'It's Mr Clough. From the school.'

A woman in the bungalow opposite had been struggling all this time to get a pushchair out of her front door, and now she shouted across:

'It's Mr Clough, you daft pig, Mr Clough from the school.'

Two children – boys 8 or 9 perhaps – had stopped and sat on the low wall, and one of them took it up too, in a singsong lah-di-dah:

'It's-Mis-tah-Cl-ough-from-the-schoo-el/Mistah-Cl-ough-from-the-schoo-el/Mis-tah.'

Then another voice – an ordinary voice, kind even – said 'Are yo'from't schoil?' and I turned in relief; at the next porch only feet away, a man had opened his door a few inches.

'Yes, yes; that's right, I'm . . .'

'Then tha' must be Mester Clough from't schoil!'

And he cracked a laugh and slammed the door.

I was in an instant frightened; I knew I had strayed across some tracks and I was frightened – not by the man, but by the power singing around me. I had no language here, no voice, and without language no power.

'I'll come back in an hour, OK? I'll give you time to – you know.'

'He'll not make any more sense then, love,' the woman called.

I walked backwards treading into a bike frame (which I found later had broken the skin on my ankle). I drove off fast; and of course it was a dead-end, Kendal Way, and they were waiting for me to return. I had to turn around at the top where the houses stopped and a short field gave on to the pit head, and I had to drive past again, my eyes straight ahead, though I saw everything in perfect detail, the man still in his doorway and the woman and the children.

By the time I got to the main road I was crying.

The fear that day was a simple animal fear and it was a galvanic nothing – mere animal twitch – by the other fear that I later felt in front of Klaus's father. I was immobilized by that other fear. That was something that reached down the canal of my composure and found the ever-leaking corrosion of my father's presence.

Of course I didn't go back that day, nor actually at all until some seven months later when Klaus was leaving us with a suit of behaviours made to cover – more or less – the bare terror. (He burst a seam in that suit; years later someone told me Klaus had stabbed to death an old man who was paying him for sex.)

I arranged to see the father on my ground; I wrote to him and he came three weeks later to the school, which involved him in a three-hour and two-bus journey. We met in the interview room, Klaus, his father and me with Chrissie, a 19-year-old assistant housemother who had been with us only three weeks, but was Klaus's assigned special person.

He made no reference to what had happened that morning, maybe had no recollection of it; but he stood in the interview room – would not sit – and the point of his journey was suddenly hard to find. Klaus stood by him, and Chrissie and I – after sitting some moments – rose too. When I said, 'This is just routine, er, really', the man continued to stare silently at me so I said 'but very necessary of course, we, er, need to', but I could think of nothing that we needed to at that moment and the thought fell away into the silence, and I found myself for the second time without language before this man, but of course, knew the place as of old.

You might have said that what he had was just a simple unpolished force; but for me it was a power, granted him sheer through some contract mutely worked years before between my father and me.

He had – I think – something of my father's eyes and something of the promise of sneer always on his upper lip, but it was not these things of themselves that thrilled me though they marked the moment. Also, although fairly short, his torso and his upper arms pressed fiercely against his suit and these were maybe things about my father.

The point is that when I said, 'This is just routine, er, really,' I heard quite simultaneously – heard, that is, in an attitude of the nerves – heard him say with all the signatures of breath and tonal economy that were engines for my father:

'I have come all this way? I have put on this suit and taken two buses? Am I right: tell me? And this is: routine. This is: routine.'

He needed no sound nor so much as a shake of the head to say this: I had done it for him, running ahead of the event to situate myself before my father. However, it was when I saw him with Klaus that I was of a moment bound utterly to him. Chrissie said – nicely, and reaching down to stroke across Klaus's brow – Chrissie said:

'Tell Dad about the puppets we made, eh?'

'We made some puppets, Dad,' Klaus said automatically.

'Did you now?'

Klaus was looking down and his father pulled his head up roughly by the chin. Disturbed in this way, Klaus's face clicked into a mad smirk of self-consciousness and his eyes were bright with their distant occupation.

'Where is it, then, this puppet?' the man asked. Then Klaus said:

'Puppet-in-c'assroom,' in a mock baby-speak.

His father was still, his jaws locked in harness of himself so that the very fat of his cheeks was rivelled with muscle. Chrissie said:

'It's lovely, really lovely, he worked very hard, didn't you, mm? He's going to give it to his sister he says.'

Klaus had no sister. There was perfect silence for maybe as much as six or eight seconds. Klaus was beaming like mad and his eyes were a merry fury. He suddenly turned to his father, and was clamouring:

'We are going to buy that Capri, aren't we Dad? Dad, are we?'

This was the saddest art I ever thought to see.

And hear me say blithely: Pity is the feeling which arrests the mind in the presence of whatsoever is grave and constant in human suffering, and unites it with the human sufferer; terror is the feeling which arrests the mind in the presence of whatsoever is grave and constant in human suffering, and unites it with the secret cause.

Watching him go off up the lane for the bus, his only son left in this school for damaged boys. Poor man; he must himself have been fighting some vestige of memory of love and warmth; and must be damaged so much; and must like me not know who he is when it comes to love. Certain postures, certain roles we can manage – a man, a lecturer, a miner – we can do these things inside a certain identity which comes with them; but inside love, where you're really on your own, where love's own dynamism and structure should hold and guide and lead, oh no, we are beggars, opportunists, scavengers, tricksters: because love's own rules – love's spontaneous, natural rules, love's intuitive rules, were taken out, beaten out of us, and in their place were put other rules: guilt, fear, recrimination.

And tricks of silence, exile and cunning.

[A version of this story was first published as P. Clough (1996) 'Again, fathers and sons': the mutual construction of self, story and special educational needs, *Disability and Society*, 11(1): 71–81.]

4 | Molly

Tim Booth asked me: *How do you give a voice to people who lack words?*

My problem with Molly is not that he *lacks* words, but rather that they can spill out of him with a wild, fairground pulse; they are sparklers, he waves them splashing around him. And my other problem with Molly's words is that many of them are not very nice; they are squibs that make you jump out of the way. For the moment I think that these are my only problems.

I have been sitting with Molly for some 10 minutes and he has explained why the pond at Tenby Dale has been closed for restocking. The tale is so parochial, has such artless warmth and polish that I feel that Molly and I are like something out of *Kes*. I think I am quite skilled at not patronizing the Mollies, so I don't entirely aspirate my h's, but I think that Molly will know somehow that I'm all right or 'o'reet'. I would want him to say to his mates, *e's o'reet that researcher bloke – 'im wi t'leather jacket*. But at this, my first meeting with Molly, I am unprepared for the sudden lash that I later come to know him by. So – and God knows where this comes from – I find myself of a moment saying

'Look here, Molly: you're intelligent, you're bright, you could . . .'

and I don't finish my sentence before Molly raps:

'What an' become a twat like thee? No offence but common sense/self-defence/off-a dat fence what? – what?'

And my audience with Molly is over for today. He is already on his feet and moving *through*, somehow – rather than round – the desks between him and the door. No longer Billy Casper, he has become Anthony Burgess's – Alex? – of *Clockwork Orange* – *Widdy-widdy-widdy-boom-boom*, and his hands beat a tattoo on the desks as he passes them. *Widdy-widdy-widdy.*

I notice that I am disappointed at being called a 'twat'.

Molly is 15 years old, nearly 16 when I meet him. His face bears traces of a prettiness that he will soon properly lose as his complexion yields fully to adolescence; for the moment, though, let him still be pretty, though his voice is at odds: mostly broken (though still sometimes – in excitement, I come to learn – there are light flecks in with the gravel).

His name is Francis Molinetti, and there are a number of reasons why I appear to pick him out from John Francis (Tosser), Des Bailey, Ginner, Mong, Tom McPhee (Toffee) and a host of indifferent others. The first of these reasons – when I think about it – has to have something to do with Molly's brightness. You can see this in his face, but not in *this* sort of brow, *that* sort of nose, or a sparkling eye, or any such. Unless it closes down – and just occasionally it does – this face is simply open with mirth. At 9 he would have looked mischievous; at 15 he is not yet watchful – though this will surely come later, after careful and before baleful; these things, too, are written in his face – no, he is not yet watchful so much as alert to possibility.

When I visit his home to meet his mother, I am amused by the identical downy moustache that they share. With her, his face loses all its nascent adult shapes, and becomes in all sincerity an artless peasant – Mario Rapuello, say – as he gazes at her with love and – not at all shy in my presence – ducks and recoils with glee from her softly cuffing him.

> 'Wha' ah do, eh? *(cuff)* Wha' ah do Mr Clough, eh? *(cuff)* Ah buy 'im a bice! Eh? *(cuff)* Ah buy 'im a bice an' wha' 'e do, eh? *(cuff)* 'E *(cuff)* sell *(cuff)* 'e! 'E sell 'e!'

I think that Mrs Molinetti has at some point bought Molly a bike, which he has sold. Molly, however, is full of glee; he is a young boy laughing, an old man crying, and she pulls his head on to her bosom, and even this does not compromise his joy at the scolding.

'I bought him a bike'. *Bice* might be a good try under other circumstances, except that Mrs Molinetti has been in England for nearly 50 years, and has roughly knit a patois – threads of West Yorkshire across a stronger, Milanese yarn – which serves her sufficiently to deal with the cone-salesmen and the women on the market. Otherwise, it seems, she has little need of English, for her family is plentiful in this city.

> 'Wha' you goin' do wi' 'im, eh? 'E goes a Youth [club] in a new trouse, 'e comes 'ome in a jean is not 'is, eh? So where you trouse, eh? I say him: Franny where you trouse, eh? An' 'e say: "Ah don't know, mam" [*ah doornt naw mam*].'

Molly is delighted with this telling off, and I am again surprised at his ease in this revelation to me.

> 'Wha' we goin' do wi' 'im, eh?'

She looks at him as if he is the most beautiful and successful man she has ever known; and he looks up in a rueful cliché at her through his long eyelashes. I witness this freight – between man and woman – with some embarrassment. I am here because I want to know how Molly's family are dealing with his exclusion from school, but it is now clear not only that Mrs Molinetti doesn't know he is excluded – and how has he managed that one? – but that in any event we should not have been able to find a shared tongue to pass either the time of day or judgement on Molly.

As Molly is seeing me to the door, I say:

'She doesn't know, does she?' and Molly smiles and looks me full in the eye.

[*I am back in the school on Wednesday, and when I go to Time Out, Tosser, Des, Toffee and Gin are vicious.*]

'Tha'rt a snake, thee,' says Des, pointing a charged contempt down his finger at me.

'Fuckin' snake,' adds Gin.

The teacher – whom I have not seen before – makes a limp effort at quietening the boys, but may as well not be there. I start to explain who I am, but realize that she doesn't want or need to know.

'Tha' stuffed 'im reet, tha' did.'

'We ain't talkin' to thee no more.'

'Tha'rt a snake, thee,' adds Mong, looking to affiliate with this choler, but draws instead a phlegm to himself; Toffee hawks and gobs directly onto Mong's workbook.

'Shut tha' fuckin' gob, Mong.'

Tosser throws a full-sized clay model football boot at Mong, which hits him behind his ear (though does not break until it hits the floor).

'They're not normally like this . . .' the teacher starts feebly, taking me for – what? – an inspector?

Gin finds me out at lunchtime as I am leaving the staff room.

'Sir . . .'

'Don't call me sir, Gin; it's Pete.'

'Molly, sir . . . Pete, sir. 'Is brother beat 'im up after you'd been, Monday. It's why he's not 'ere today, 'e shoulda been back today, right? Lol, Lolly. Beat 'im up reet, 'as a face like mince beef, sir.'

'Lol?'

'Lolly's 'is brother, sir. Runs the business. 'As a personal number plate.'

The head of the business – Molly's elder brother by 17 years – is called Lolly; not, actually, because it is an ice cream business, but because he was christened Lorenzo.

[*I interview Molly.*]

> Molly: It's the only language 'e 'ad. It's the only thing 'e knew. Wham! Bang! Lol's the same.
>
> PC: Lol?
>
> M: Lolly, me brother Lolly. Language of the fist. Smack first, ask later.
>
> PC: Does Lol . . . did Lol get it? I mean when he was little.
>
> M: Oh God, ay. When 'e was big, too – 18, 19. I've seen 'im push Lol through t'shed door. Lol came back from't round – van round – 60p down or summat, and 'e just smacked him – wham! – and he went through't shed door. Not as much as me, though. 'E 'ated me cos I could speak, I used to speak . . .
>
> PC: How d'you mean 'speak'?
>
> M: I used to answer 'im back. Like 'e'd say: 'You think you're so bloody smart, eh?' An' I'd say summat like [*in mock-posh voice*]: 'I'm reasonably well provided for above the neck, father' – an' 'e'd go bloody bonkers – Wham! Wham! Smack-bloody-smack!
>
> PC: What . . . you mean you knew? That he'd hit you?
>
> M: Oh aye, yeh, course. It was my only defence against him – words, 'e 'ated words, me dad did, 'ated 'em.
>
> PC: So you wound him up with words . . . and he'd then hit you?
>
> M: Something like that. Yeh, summat like that.
>
> PC: Why?
>
> M: [*after a long pause . . . 10 seconds?*] Survival? [*Appears to think about this . . . then*] Yeh: survival. I learned to lie to survive.

A week or so later he stops me in the corridor and thrusts a paper at me; it's torn from a school poetry anthology. '*That's a bit what it was, what it was like*', he mutters (without lips) and is gone and within seconds I can hear him way down the corridor, become Alex again: *Widdy-widdy-widdy . . .*

The torn page is Ephraim Moras's 'Bowl of Fruit':

a small child, less than table-height,
is reaching for an apple on the table;
every time his fingers near the apple, a fist smashes down on his fingers;

one time he touches the apple even,

and the fist smashes him in the face,
sending his head hard against the architrave behind him.

From the floor a theory of apples starts like this.

[*Mr Desborough is 51 and is deputy headteacher.*]

Mr D: We are talking one nasty piece of work, just that: a nasty piece of work.

PC: Was he always, I mean when . . .

Mr D: Something happens. His first year he was all right. Obscure but all right. I'll tell you what though, we take all the Year 9 to the Lakes at Easter, well Carlisle but, Molinetti shat in a staff sleeping bag.

PC: Shat?

Mr D: We were all out for the evening, a sort of wide game, you know and he came back to the huts and he shat, he deliberately well you couldn't accidentally, he actually, went in one of the staff huts, he shat in this, in Mark's sleeping bag. Had rolled it down, shat, zipped it back up, put the pillow job back. Mark gets into bed, I was there, wriggles down – yeugggh!

PC: Mark Hedley? What did you do/how was he dealt with?

Mr D: Oh there was no proof, we couldn't do anything. Short of having a path lab report on the turd, you couldn't prove anything. But you see he would know that, Molinetti. Oh we're dealing with a clever one here, make no mistake.

PC: Ah but he *is* clever, isn't he? I think he . . .

Mr D: No, not really. He's not really clever. He's learned a few tricks is all, a few tricks of language it's true, he has it's true. Have you spoken to Mark, Mark Hedley? Yeh? Well Mark will tell you, he's told you I'm sure, that Molinetti is a misunderstood . . . a misunderstood *hero*. Molinetti is a bad lot is all, I'm afraid. One bad lot.

PC: Yeh, Mark does think a lot of him.

Mr D: D'you know what Molinetti thinks of Mark? Mark who champions him, St Mark who – look this is between us but Mark who'd, no I can say it, I can, I'll own to it . . . Mark has this thing about reaching out to kids, speaking but really speaking to them and Molinetti plays him like a kite, like a kite. Mark refused to believe that it was Molinetti shat in his sleeping bag, wouldn't have it. Now ask yourself, ask me, ask *why* would Molinetti shit in Hedley's sleeping bag? Answer that, eh? Well, I'll tell you, he was appalled he was just *appalled* to be championed by a fag . . . he was just appalled, it's as simple as that.

[*Two days later; 10.45 a.m. Molly and the other boys are waiting in Time Out for Mr Stephenson head of year.*]

> *Molly:* Ilkley: what a fuckin' place to grow up in, eh? 'Ave yer ever bin? I tell yer.
> *Gin:* 'Arrogate.
> *Des:* Fuckin' 'arrogate.
> *G:* York.
> *D:* Fuckin' York.
> *G:* Whitby.
> *D:* Fuckin' Shitby.
> [*Laughter; inaudible*]

> *M:* . . . near this joke-shop, reet [*right*]? and traffic-warden, Paki reet? says [*in caricatured pan-Asian dialect:*] 'You must not be parrr-king here, oh no, oh my goodness gracious no, innit?' Reet? 'n our Lol, reet? he says—
> [*Noise/chaos as Des falls backwards off desk*]
> *D:* Tha' pushed me fuck-face.
> *G:* Ah fuckin' didn't.
> *D:* Tha' fuckin' did, tha' fuckin' dees [*dies*] thee, tha' does, tha' fuckin' wait . . .

It goes on; it goes on and on; it goes on and on and on and how it wearies; its tired, routine ugliness actually makes you tired; it sucks the life from the room.

Mr Stephenson enters. He knows I'm with the boys and (correctly) ignores me. The boys sort-of stand.

> *Mr S:* Sit down, lads. What happened/Don't all talk at once. Ginner?
> *G:* I weren't even there, Sir.
> *M:* 'E weren't. Sir, somebody put it in his bag.
> *Mr S:* Shut up for a minute, Molinetti.
> *M:* But 'e weren't, Sir, it's not just.
> *Mr S:* Just, Molly? Tell me about justice, then.
> *M:* Sir it's not reet, Govinder did it 'n put it in Gin's bag. Sir, it's always the same if it's a Paki. Sir.
> *Mr S:* D'you want to think about what you just said, Molinetti?
> *M:* No sir, it's true sir, t'Pakis always get away wi' it.
> *Mr S:* Right, Molinetti and Ginner stay here, the rest of you get off to class.

[*Turning to me*] I wonder if you'd mind leaving us as well?

[*I interview Mark Hedley, Molly's form tutor.*]

Mark Hedley says, 'Ooh, that Salma Fariq! Ooh,' he says, 'Ooh, she's *aw*-ful!' And his wrist flops away to the right as his head tosses to the left with the slightest '*ter*'. I can't believe this the first time I meet him, and he excites in me a dismissive scorn. He is 5 foot 4 – no more – and dressed top to toe in black, trailing the fashion by a few years, but making a strong point for all that. His shirt is black with a very narrow charcoal tie. He has two tiny silver sleepers in each of his ears.

MH: It's 'cos I look young, I do have some difficulties, but then I don't too, if you know what I mean. I get on very well – very well – with children who have problems both academically and otherwise socially. I get on very well for some reason with the roughs, the very badly behaved, I get on with them very well indeed. I get satisfaction from watching them achieve something that they wouldn't otherwise.

PC: If someone stood back and looked at what you were doing, what would they say was happening? What would they identify . . . as the things that made it possible for you to get on well with those . . .

MH: tough guys and—

PC: Yeh.

MH: I think one of the reasons I get on with them is because I was exactly the same when I was at school. I was expelled from school because of my behaviour and stuff and I'm still quite young [26] and I can identify still with what's going on. I know how I was treated at school but there's no way, there's no way that I would ever treat anybody in the same way . . .

[*Later*] . . . the school I went to, I mean the whole attitude of the place stank as far as I was concerned. The teachers were appalling. If they came to a school like this they'd be dead within a week because they couldn't actually teach. I got picked on a lot, I can't tell you how awful it was. *Aw*ful! And I can tell you – *well* – I've never been one to take things easily if I don't agree. I'm quite an independent person and I just started acting up all the time and being really destructive, did no work, I was a punk and all this sort of thing. I dyed my hair, wouldn't wear school uniform, all that sort of thing, in the end they just asked me to go, much to my mum's *ut*ter dismay and horror. Then I came here and loved it and settled in straight away.

PC: What, you came to this school?

MH: Yeh, I . . .

PC: I mean – as a pupil?

MH: Yes, I came into the fifth year.

PC: Wow . . . I . . .

MH: And it's part of why I get on with the kids, 'cos I know what it's like both sides of the fence, you know? And I am still young, that's important.

PC: You said that before, is it very important to you, that?

MH: Oh yes, oh yes, yes. I think here with me being quite young looking I find that pupils – not just from my own form but from other forms as well – they just come and chat and talk either about a problem or they'll just come for a chat or a joke. I find that really helps being young and . . . sometimes I find I'm in a bit of an awkward position because they are trying to get me to side with them against other teachers and stuff and that's really difficult, especially when I agree with what they're saying. I find that happens quite a lot.

PC: Does anyone get upset about your dress, the way you dress?

MH: Oh I'm surprised I've not been sacked! I'm quite happy with what I am, it works well for me and I get through to the kids which is the most important.

PC: Do you feel any criticism, any explicit criticism of how you look, how you dress, what you are, whatever . . .

MH: Yes from some people. I wear the ear-rings, funny shoes perhaps. Some people would probably think it's not a suitable way for a teacher to look. But me . . . well, I'd rather be around the kids, anyway. I would say that the people I empathize most with here are the children. That sounds a bit corny, I know, but I'd much rather be with them than the staff most of the time. I still feel young at heart, that's another corny thing to say but I still feel very youthful. There're lots of ways I feel very old too but I like to sit down and talk about music and stuff and I think what kids do is exciting and what they are is exciting and you see all the potential in them. I think I've made a lot of mistakes in my life and I don't want them to do the same, the same sort of things.

[*Later/another day*]

MH: I don't really judge kids you see, I get angry if I'm rubbed up the wrong way but the kids know I'm not going to go ape-poo! Like the other day when [head of science] sent a child, Molinetti, to me

PC: Ah, Molly!

MH: You've met Molly, Molly's great, fierce, fiercely bright and—

PC: How do you get on with Molly? Does Molly—

MH: he's me is Molly, just like me. We're like two animals sort of sniffing round each other, mutual respect, he wouldn't come too close but he wouldn't stay too far away, he—

PC: Why was he sent to you?

MH: Knows his boundaries. Oh [science teacher] can't stand kids as bright as himself, I don't know, Molly said something. I mean, *fancy* a 50-year-old man having to send *a* 15-year-old child to a 26-year-old form tutor because he was *cheeky*!

PC: What did you do, to Molly?

MH: Oh talked to him then there's a procedure, he had to go to Time Out for the rest of the morning.

PC: Tell me, I mean tell me more about Molly . . .

MH: Molly's a delight. Like I say, Molly's me. Bright as a button . . . Molly's a classic . . . a *classic* . . .

[*I 'interview' Molly again.*]

M: Where shall I start?

PC: Did you have trouble at [primary school]?

M: No, not much.

PC: Not much?

M: No. Not much.

PC: Like how much?

M: Not much.

PC: Like . . . what? What did you do, get in trouble for?

M: [*Deadpan*] I set fire to the cleaners.

PC: The cleaners . . . what?

M: ⎰The cleaners, there were two cleaners and they were 'avin' a fag.

PC: ⎱You set fire . . .

M: ⎰In this den, reet? Caretaker's den, reet?

PC: ⎱you mean to the cleaners themselves?

M: [*Ploughing on regardless* . . .] 'n' I set fire to this waste-paper basket, reet 'n' it all went up . . . brrrrrumppphhh! [*from clasped hands, mimes the centrifugal explosion, and rolls a growling crescendo in his throat before the big, big labial plosive; he likes this effect, and repeats it, improving his performance, and then a third time, hands finally high above his head configuring dancing flames* . . .]

PC: [*Eventually, and laughing, possibly too much*] Gosh! Wow, some event, eh? And were the cleaners in the room, the den?

M: Don't be fuckin' soft.

[*A long silence; maybe nearly a full minute*]

PC: I got into some right scrapes when I was at school . . .

[*Silence; Molly straightfaced now, watching through the window the soccer on the field*]

PC: D'you want to – shall we leave it for today, then?

[*Silence; Molly suddenly bangs the window hard with his forefinger several times*]

M: [*Shouting*] Pass the fuckin' thing! Pass it! Pass it! Pass it! Oh fuck, Anderson! [*As the player is – easily – dispossessed, 'Anderson' immediately picks up a small clod of mud and throws it towards 'our' window. It misses, but . . .*]

The scene takes on *Kes* again, for the small, tubby middle-aged Brian Glover of a teacher who is the referee runs shouting towards us . . .

BG: Molinetti! Molinetti! Open that window! Now, Molinetti! [*He sees me and says, no jot less quietly*] He's with you is he?
PC: Yes, I'm.
BG: He's with you, right, right Molinetti. [*Word by word pushed with his forefinger almost up to Molly's nose*] KEEP–YOUR–BIG–ITALIAN–NOSE–OUT.
M: Racist, sir, that's racist, you 'eard 'im didn't yer?. Racist.

For a moment, a tiny moment, the Brian Glover man is quite without doubt going to seize Molly by something; doesn't, in fact, because – true to this film script we seem to be making here – his class is now alert to the show and is in tumult.

Class: Molly! Eye-tie-shite-eye! 'Oo's yer friend in the leathers, Molly? [*Which is me*] Molinetti wanker! Molly's gorra friend . . .
M: [*Shouting inches from 'Mr Glover's' ear*] Tha' dees [*dies*], Pitcher, tha' fuckin' dees! 'Ah'll fuckin' tek thee out, cunt . . .
BG: Right, Molinetti, Molinetti go on, get to the Head, go on – to the Head, no, Molinetti, that's enough, go on, now, Molinetti, go on
M: You're fuckin' dead, Pitcher.
BG: [*Raising a leg onto the windowsill*] Go on! Go on, Molinetti! I said to the Head, Molinetti [*Climbing through the window, even!*] That's it, go on! Go on! [*He is through the window and is pushing Molly; gently, but pushing. Molly catches the untied lace of a trainer beneath the other foot, and stumbling, raises a hand to right himself. Mr Glover steps back in alarm, and, to me*] You saw him! You saw that! You've done it now, Molinetti! Oh, you've done it now.

And to my strange delight, Molly – seeing the gallows before him anyway – appears to think: 'All right, I might as well take something with me' and pops Glover neatly in the nose. Glover drops quite simply, though squealing. For Molly's career this is a new turn.

[*Two days later; waiting at the bus stop. The excluded Molly has come to meet his mates at the gates.*]

Tosser: Is it on?
PC: Yes it's on.

Tosser: Can I say owt?

PC: If you want, but—

Tosser: Fuck! Fuckfuckfuckfuck! Shitarsefuckfuck!

Gin: Tha'rt sad, thee, Tosser.

Toffee: Play it back, sir, go on play it back.

PC: It's . . . OK [*I rewind the tape, and replay*].

Gin: Tha' sounds like a girl, thee! [*Mimics in falsetto*] Fuckfuckfuck.

Molly: Tha'rt the fuckin' girl, pin-prick. Tha' could shag a louse tha' could.

Toffee: 'Ere: tha' knows Netto. reet? Well Netto reckons Gin shags Fatima, reet?

Gin: [*Laughing*] Fuckin' didn't. [*Turning to Mong*] Tha' shags geese, dun't tha' Mong?

[*Group 'turns' to Mong*]

Molly: Goose gobbles 'im more like. [*Seizes microphone from my hand, and starts a whispered and minutely accurate David Attenborough imitation*] Here we see the . . . baby Mong, *Mongo Mongo*, the infant Mong, . . . under some considerable threat from . . . the other animals . . . I can see the adult Tosser there, *Tossus Tossus* . . . [*The others are trying to force Mong's head down to a dog turd on the pavement*] But wait, wait! The Researcher – a fine beast in his leather jacket, the corduroy trouser . . . in green/a *dark* green/yes – the Researcher is approaching! What law . . . what . . . ancient . . . law of the jungle is at work here? The bold . . . the . . . *manly* researcher . . . oh! He *rescues* the infant Mong! Oh what a *fine* beast this is! [*etc.*]

Karen, my research assistant, couldn't stand working on the project, and left as soon as she could get a 'real' job. But she kept in touch with Mark Hedley – really liked him – and I think they 'did' clubs and things. Anyway when I saw her last year, she told me this story: Mark and two – women – friends were crossing Halifax Lane at about one in the morning, Sunday morning, they'd been to a club or something and were walking down into town in search of something to eat. Of three lads some 50 yards behind them, one started calling: '*Oy queer/oy bumboy/oy you fuckin' queer/oy fuckarse.*' His friends seemed to try to quiet him. Mark and the women walked on, and the man called on and on. '*Fuck-arse/Brownknob/Pervert.*' The man suddenly detached himself from his friends, who turned a corner and were gone; the man ran hard up to Mark from behind and pushed him round. '*Ent tha gonna say nowt shagarse? Eh? As tha nowt to say for theesen pervert?*' The man rolled a gob of phlegm in his throat – slowly, clearly – and then shot it hard onto Mark's face, where it hit on the corner of his mouth. One of the women punched – or made to punch – the man in his face but was too slow; he kicked her legs from under her and stamped on her as she fell beneath him; and then he beat up the three of them, swiftly and wildly. They lay almost without moving on the pavement for some whole minutes before a car stopped and help was sent for.

At the hospital the police were keen to take statements but Mark and the women were silent and would say nothing; the police were formally polite at first and finally – convinced that Mark knew but was protecting his attacker – derisive. They threw the fag and his dykes out at 3.40 a.m.

[A version of this story was first published as 'Molly: some indices of disturbed/ disturbing voices', in P. Clough and L. Barton (1998) *Articulating with Difficulty: Research Voices in Inclusive Education*. London: Sage.]

5 | Rob

When Rob Joynson was 43 he came into school on a Tuesday morning much as usual; and passing at 10.40 by a maths class taken by Michelle G. – a probationer of 23 – and hearing terrible noise; and seeing through the window a boy at the back fetch a fat gob on Michelle's back as she walked down the aisle smiling, smiling too, too nervously, her hands doing 'Down, please: down, down' at the noise; seeing this marbled yellow gob on Michelle's ordinary blouse on her decent body, Rob Joynson rushed into the room and to the back and took the boy – Mark something – by the ears, both ears, and pulled him up out of – through almost – his desk and repeatedly smashed his head against a chart of tessellations on the wall. And Michelle pulled at him from behind and screamed, and he twisted the boy down by his ears and pushed at him with his foot, kicking until he was quite under the desk. Then Rob started to cry and there was terrible silence – where there had been terrible noise – but for Rob searching for breath to fuel the small fearful wails which broke from him. When – thank God – someone laughed finally, unable to stay with the pain a moment longer, Rob fled the room.

By 11.30 he was at home, his wife and his family doctor were expected shortly, and he was carefully drying the pots on the draining-board. Rose Thorpe, the headteacher, was putting the mugs on the hooks beneath the wall-cupboards. Rob had not spoken – not a word – since Rose had fetched him from the caretaker's 'den'; the caretaker had run to the office to say that RJ – as most people knew him in the school – was crying, no *wailing* in the den; was, well: *barmy.*

'Rob . . . Rob, you know you shouldn't . . . O Rob, Rob, dear Rob. Look, let me . . .'

and she made to wipe his nose with kitchen roll but – though he offered no resistance – she stopped at his smile which excluded her so clearly from his occupation.

'I had this one' – holding a mug celebrating the Miners' Strike of '84.

Rose is very short, short and quite round. When finally she feels she must, on pain of rebuke, *must* touch him, she reaches up to his face quite as he is launched into a gesture – actually the first expression of his presence – turning both hands outward at the wrist; and she walks each of her breasts perfectly into his hands. And then they laugh; and then hold – close – and then Rose is crying and Rob is calm.

The first words from Rob, each as flat as the next, an even pause between each:

'What/ever/shall/I/do/Rose'

Rob was deputy headteacher at an 11–18 comprehensive school serving about 1500 students. Rob was recruited as head of special educational needs (SEN) ten years previously; actually became really noticeable in a pastoral role; and moved naturally to the post of deputy (welfare) at a time when the school was particularly turbulent.

[*A day later, Rob is visited by Dave Bird, a teachers' union representative at his school.*]

D: Look Rob. I wanted you to know that we're going to take this one up. We're really going to run with it. We're with you, Rob. This is the one we've been waiting for. We can win this; *you* can win this.

R: I'm not sure. I've been thinking. I don't know what to do.

D: Look, man: you can't drop it now. This – this – is what we've been waiting for. Not waiting five, seven years; waiting – working – all our bloody professional lives, man! Don't you see it? You didn't hit Mark Whatisname. Ok, yes all right sure you hit him but – and this is the point, Rob: the system's been hitting him – and what's more you – relentlessly for years. We're the thin chalk line, man. What was at work in you that day was years – fucking *eons*, man – of a repressive system. A system that we – it's us, Rob – a system that we support. What would happen if we didn't? Fucking chaos, man! Chaos! And it did; look: what happened on that day was: you said: enough, no more, that's it, this will not do. All right, a kid got hurt; you got hurt, man. But do you see? You blew the whistle on all the shit. Oh this is going to be big – big, big, big!

Rob – standing propped against the sink – Rob said without life:

'Dave you know as well, better than I do that the local authority won't let it happen, they won't.'

D: Robert the Authority is fucked backwards. They are screwed, absolutely fucked . . . this Authority has feared this for years. They've kept resources from us, they've stinted, they've scrooged on

Special Ed. You know it, man! And now they're getting their own, they're going to get their fucking own! I'm going to enjoy this.

There was silence for nearly half a minute. Then Rob said – said like words punctured of meaning, so flat:

R: Dave: I hit the kid. I kicked him. I trampled on him.
D: Says who?
R: Says I, Dave; I know. And 30 kids know. And Michelle knows.
D: Nobody's going to listen to the kids against you; anyway there's no kids going to speak up for Mark is what I hear. The kids know what you are, Rob. They love you. Mark was bad news for them and you, too. Look: I looked up his record – hang on a minute – d'you know how many times he's been suspended since he's been in secondary school? Do you know how many times he's been referred to the whole gang of people at County Hall – psychs, support, Alternative Curriculum, Family Support Group, Welfare Officers. Do you know his court record?

Bird opened his bag and made to bring out a file, but Rob stopped him.

R: I know. They're my files, right?
D: Rob, that kid would've been out last year if the lovely Sister Rosemary hadn't been so fucking fearful about her record as Mrs Liberal-we-can-deal-with-every-little-shit at County Hall. This kid has a history – a *history*, Rob – of assault.
R: That's not fair, Dave, and not true. Nothing was proven last year and well you know it.

Bird was silent for a few seconds. Then he began quietly:

D: Some of the kids – I won't say who at the moment, right? – some of the kids say he put his hand up Michelle's skirt a couple of weeks ago . . .
R: Dave, get out! Get right out! Go on, out this is shit, pure shit, you know it is . . .
D: Rob wait: wait, man. It happened, and these kids are prepared to say it.
R: If it happened Michelle would have said something. Why didn't Michelle say something?

Bird spread his palms, who-knows? but also, with his eyebrows: you-know, and, with a little smile: I-know.

D: Rob you know my views on kids like this. We cannot – fuck it we *will* not – go the final mile on kids who are too fucked up for what we *can* do. It's not fair on anybody, Rob. I don't need to rehearse this with you. We are talking a kid who yes, sure, has great problems. But at some point someone has got to have the fucking wit and the balls to say: No, no fucking way, this far and no fucking further, man! Out out out! Rob, it's the only way we'll make an impression on . . . on County Hall for a start. Rosie should have done that and done it two years ago. As it is it was left to you. Or rather you were left to it. You're the victim, Robert. Not Mark, not Michelle . . .

R: Dave, I'm tired . . . can we leave it for a while?

D: Sure, sure, sure. Sorry to go on, man, sorry. It's just . . . just wholly historical. It's not you, Rob, whatever happens it's not you. You and me and Mark Thing are just caught up in this thing playing through us. Look, you can't see this, right, but it's our privilege, man; it's our privilege to witness now for everything we stand for. You won't live with yourself if you don't witness now, Rob . . .

R: Dave, I . . .

D: Sorry . . . look I'm going.

At the door Bird turned again.

D: I've got the *Guardian* phoning this afternoon. Not going to deal with the right-wing shit press. And that little fuck from the *Gazette*'s been nosing around like a dog looking for shit. We're going to speak to the *Guardian*, no others. Rob?

R: Mm?

D: If they'll come – probably send someone from Manchester – you'll speak to the *Guardian*, won't you? I think tomorrow or Thursday. We've got to be pro-active on this one, keep it moving. We're behind you, Rob; you mustn't let us down.

Bird squeezed Rob's shoulder hard and it was as good an excuse as any for Rob's wet eyes. Bird looked big with solidarity:

'I know, man, I know. Hang on in there.'

(But) Rob was snailing trails through the condensation on the window. In the garden the dirty residue of snow still highlighted the depressions in the lawn.

[*The following day, Rob's wife Jan returns from her work (also as a teacher).*]

'What are you doing? Rob, what are you doing?'

Jan has just come through the front door and stands with her briefcase against the open doorway. Rob stops dialling and puts the phone down.

J: Darling? [*Darling* – where did *that* come from?] Darling, who are you calling?

R: It doesn't matter.

J: Rob, for the first time in – what? two days? – you pick up a phone . . . No: you initiate a contact, you actually try to communicate with someone; and you say it doesn't matter? Come on, Rob, be bloody fair.

Jan follows Rob into the kitchen where he stands against the sink (and Jan realizes for the first time that Rob is nearly always in the kitchen now, nearly always standing against the sink).

R: Michelle is going to testify against me.

J: And you were going to—

R: I don't know what I was going to do. I wanted to speak to her.

J: The little cow. The horrid little cow, the—

R: No. She's right, she's right. The facts are there. Teachers-should-not-beat-children-up, right? What hope is there if a 23-year-old doesn't insist on that? She's right through and through. And you'd be defending her if you could set me aside for one moment.

J: All right I shouldn't call her a cow, I'm sorry, that's unforgivable. OK? But she's wrong, she'll send you to the gallows on a principle she can't possibly – can't *remotely* – understand.

R: Jan: she has integrity; she has commitment; she's a good kid, she'll be a good teacher.

J: Was there something between you?

Jan took a single glass and poured herself a drink.

R: How do you mean?

J: Oh. I see.

R: No. You see nothing. Don't do that, Jan, don't fucking do that. I'm her mentor, you know that, it's my job in their first year. I like her and maybe – at first – maybe she was – I don't know – attracted; but no, there was nothing. Don't do that, Jan.

J: She was attracted, oh yes, with her pushy little tits under her pretty little print blouses and her ear-to-ear twinkle and—

R: Oh for fuck's sake, Jan.

J: Oh for God's sake, Rob. You've no bloody idea, have you, you don't know the first bloody thing. Little things like Michelle know exactly – precisely down to the last detail – what they do to semi-reconstructed, guilty liberal men like you. And you fall for it, don't you.

R: Jan, there was nothing.

J: Rob, there was something. Why did you go in there that day? Tell me: have you never seen things like that before? Why should some . . . some wretch, some scrap like Mark Thing have to get it in the neck because some Michelle – the lovely Michelle. Little pretty-blouse-bitch Michelle.

R: Jan, this is crazy. I never touched her, for God's sake.

J: Of course you didn't, that's not the point. The point – actually – is just that you didn't know what you were doing when you burst in that day but sure as hell you were driven by something.

R: Suddenly . . . suddenly I have drives that I don't know the first fucking thing about! First there's my therapist and apparently my mother is driving me; then there's Dave Bird and the whole of western capitalism is working through me if I did but know it; now you and it seems my prick knows something I don't. You're all so busy fucking inventing me, where am I in all this, eh?

Rob smashed his fist down on the draining-board and a teaspoon bounced down onto the floor. Silence. Jan said quietly

'We haven't spoken so much for months.'

[*In the end it was Jan who rang Michelle.*]

J: Is that Michelle? Michelle, this is Jan.

M: Oh. Mrs Joynson, yes, hello.

J: *Mrs,* Michelle? And anyway I've always been Hirst. *Miss* Hirst.

M: Sorry, you took me by surprise. I hadn't expected to hear. From you.

J: Sure, I understand. Look, I don't want to intimidate you, I just want to ask you if you're sure you know what you're doing.

M: Mrs . . . Jan, I can't discuss this, I've been told not to talk about this.

J: I know that, Michelle. I won't try to pretend: of course I'd like to persuade you to drop it all. I live with it all the time, Michelle, this man who's like an empty house, like, like . . . a deserted squat.

M: Jan, don't do this to me.

J: Michelle, don't do this to Rob. He's a fine teacher, you know that, Michelle, he's a good man. Michelle, schools need men like Rob.

M: Jan, I can't do this I must hang up, I'm going to hang up.

J: Michelle, please . . . please listen: Rob needs . . .

Jan refilled her glass, and remained standing by the silent phone.

[*Rose Thorpe visits Mark's parents at their home.*]

'We don't want no trouble, Mrs Thorpe, we've had enough trouble.'

Rose put her cup down by her bag at her feet, and waited.

'He's not a bad lad, Mrs Thorpe, he's really not, you know.'

'He's 5 foot 4 now, you know,' said Mark's father.

They were obviously heavy smokers, but were not smoking in Rose's presence. When Rose said: 'Do you mind if I smoke?' they all laughed – eagerly, really – and offered cigarettes, each turning to the others and pushing forward the cigarette packet.

'Go on, go on; no, no; oh all right but you must have one of mine in a minute! There now that's better. We smoke too much, don't we?'

There was some silence as they smoked together. Finally, Mark's mother spoke.

Mother: What will happen, Mrs Thorpe?
Rose: There's to be an inquiry. Somebody from County. The inquiry will establish what happened in the classroom. After that—
M: But we know what happened.
R: We know some of what happened.
M: But Michelle saw it all. She says—
R: Michelle?
M: Mark's teacher. The maths teacher. She says—
R: You've seen Michelle? She's been here?
M: Oh yes, she was lovely. She's been really helpful. She came to see Mark. She brought him some work. He's been working so hard.
Father: She said we must call her Michelle.
R: Look, I can't stop Michelle coming here. I can't stop Mark seeing Michelle and – yes – it's nice of her. But it may not be a good idea right at present.
M: I don't understand . . .
R: Michelle is an excellent teacher. She's a very committed, a very caring professional. But it may not be in anybody's interest for her to . . . spend time here. There are some different views about what happened – and about what should happen now – and it could get . . . confused. Yes, we need to keep Mark supplied with work but that should be through his form tutor. I shall have a word with Michelle. Meanwhile . . .
M: Mrs Thorpe, we don't want no trouble. Mark's seen enough trouble.

[*A day later, and Dave Bird goes to see Rose Thorpe in her office.*]

D: I'll stand, thanks. I've been sat in Appeals at County Hall all morning, I'm stiff as a corpse.
R: I've got about 10 minutes, Dave, then there's—
D: Sorry, I'll get to the point. The local and regional union committees met Sunday and yesterday, extraordinary meetings. There are some differences but—
R: The point, Dave. Give me the fine tuning later.

    D: Rose, you cannot readmit that boy under these circumstances. We won't let you. No way.

Rose looked up.

    R: We? We, Dave?
    D: Rose, the staff will resist it unanimously. All but unanimously and . . . and obviously . . .
    R: That sounds like a threat. Is this a threat, Dave?
    D: Officially: no. This is a statement from the Union Rep. You know that, Rose. But unofficially, Rose . . . yes: don't do it, Rose, or hell will break out.
    R: Dave, the governors have . . . *required* that Mark be readmitted; that's what the Authority wants, too. And that is what I want, too, for that matter.
    D: And what about Rob?
    R: The position is that Rob is on indefinite sick-leave. When he is . . . better, the position will be reviewed.
    D: No way, Rose! You're selling Rob down the line! No no no way!
    R: Don't no way me, Dave. Put your hand down, sit down and listen. Right? No: listen to me for a moment. I think . . . the governors think; *we* think: if Mark is not readmitted, his parents will – almost certainly – take out a civil action against Rob, the school and probably the Authority. Don't ask me who's behind them, though someone clearly is. No: don't interrupt. Now think that through. It is a simple, medical fact that Mark has – still – a cracked rib. That's fact. Then there's Michelle. Michelle is sure of what she saw. Michelle does not waver, Dave. Michelle may be having her finest hour, but she does not waver.

Bird was silent, thinking thinking thinking.

    D: Rose, I must speak to the members. Give me 24 hours.
    R: No. I'll give you to end of school: 3.30. Then a letter – of some sort – must go, first class, to Mark's parents.

Bird was back at 3.20.

    D: Rose: we won't play. I've done what I can but the staff won't have it. If you move to readmit that boy there will be immediate and forceful action.
    R: Forceful, Dave?
    D: We shall strike . . .
    R: Regional Office . . . well, Geoff Bennett has given me his word . . .
    D: Rose, Geoff Bennett is a soft turd as well you know. I have had

authority – well, a very strong nod – from National. Bennett and Regional are irrelevant.

Rose sat back in her chair and said in a little, little voice:

R: Dave . . . Dave: does it *have* to be like this?
D: Rose, yes. YES, Rose, it does. (His volume in contrast to her small tone) I could say *Rose: does it have to be like this?* You don't *HAVE* to do this, Rose; your hands are *NOT* tied. Rob Joynson is a fucking good teacher and a fucking good deputy and a fucking good friend to YOU!

Rose was silent now for a long time. There was a knock at the door and then silence. The end-of-day bell rang shrill for 10 seconds. Finally Rose said slowly, evenly, in a grave monotone:

'*He – did – it.*'

And then, in just-so resignation:

'He did it, Dave. He did it.'

[*Rose telephones Rob.*]

Rose: Rob, I must talk to you. There's a deal.
Rob: Fire away, Rose.
Rose: I can't on the phone. Can I come round?
Rob: I should be able to fit you in . . .
Rose: See you in ten.

Rob let Rose in at the back door and then went back to the sink at the window. He made to put the kettle on but Rose shook her head, and stayed standing at the other end of the kitchen.

Rob: What's the deal?
Rose: The deal is: Mark is readmitted on Monday. Michelle goes immediately to Priory College as Acting Second in Maths. You – you are on indefinite sick-leave until you are ready to go to another post. The authority will guarantee your salary for three years though no particular status. I've got to say you're not likely to get a senior post.
Rob: All very reasonable, really.
Rose: Don't be bitter, Rob.
Rob: No. No, I won't be bitter.

Rob turned to the window again, and again started snailing trails and traces down the condensation: what remained of a treble clef, from earlier in the day, had run and there was a pool on the sill.

Rob: And if I don't accept the deal?

Rose: If you don't accept the deal, Rob . . . if you don't accept the deal you will be suspended with immediate effect, there will be a full inquiry and there is no doubt that you will be found against and dismissed. Of this there is no doubt, Rob. You must be sure of that, sure of it. You may even be prosecuted by the governors to defend any case Mark's parents might bring against the school. There's a case in Hampshire at the moment . . .

Rob: Is that all?

Rose: No, that's not all. Michelle has filed a complaint of sexual harrassment against you . . .

Rob: That's preposterous! Fucking fantastic! That's . . . that's . . . Rose . . .

Rose: I know, Rob, I really do.

Rob: Whatever did I do to that girl, Rose? Why does she hate me like this? What is it? Tell me!

Rose: I don't know. She's scared, we're all scared. Anyway: she'll drop it if you go along with the deal.

Rob: I won't, I fucking won't; I'll fight it, I'll actually fight the whole lot of it. This can't happen . . .

Rose: Rob: listen.

Rose crossed the room and (crying now) took Rob's face in her hands.

'Rob: you don't understand. They won't let you win. Do you understand? You can win – nothing. Listen to this carefully: you are not to be allowed to win anything. You are not to be allowed to go away with anything but a . . . but a salary. The price of conscience, Rob, that's what you get. The cost of our silence and the price of our conscience.'

Rose was crying openly now, blubbering her words and shaking slightly. Rob held her against his chest.

Rose straightened up. She blew her nose on some kitchen towel which Rob offered her, and went back to lean against the back door.

Rob: And where are you in all this, Rose? Will you sleep at night?

Rose was silent for maybe a full minute; then, staring at the back door as though she were reading from it she said:

'Not for a while, I think. But then: yes, I have to. We shall all have to. Even you.'

'The show must go on, eh?'

Rob turned from the window to look down the kitchen at Rose. It was now quite dark outside and in.

Rob: Rose?

Rose: I find it hard, Rob, terribly hard.

Rob: Look at me, Rose. Rose? Look at me; is it so hard to look at me?

Rose: Yes, it is. It is; very hard. There's been a lot of good feeling between us for so long but now . . . now there's a *fact* between us, forever there. I can't get round it, Rob. You know, when I talked to Michelle last week – the Blessed Michelle – she said something which I understand. She said: I didn't ask to see his violence, Rose, but now it's all of him I can see. Well, that's overblown, I know; it's part of the role she's made for herself but . . . I know what she means. The damage, the events, the physical thing of it all – all that we can get over. But the glimpse of violence . . . that unwitting glance you gave us all – and forever . . . into our own violence, Rob. It's that we can't live with.

As much as two full minutes later, Rose stirred.

'I must go.'

Rob didn't move. In the dark room it was impossible to see whether he was looking in or out the room.

'There's one more thing, Rob.'

But then Rob obviously turned, so he was facing in the room.

Rob: Can there be? Don't tell me: I'm to have my balls chopped off in assembly.

Rose: Don't joke, Rob. Listen. Dave Bird is planning action.

Rob: Action?

Rose: Unofficial strike, tomorrow. I think he'll get half, maybe two-thirds of the staff. Anyway, enough to have press, TV and everyone down here. Then everyone loses everything: you, Mark, the school, the Authority – it'll all go up. Do you follow me? It will be open, national, bloody warfare. You will be a national figure, Rob. The *Sun* will be published from your doorstep. You must stop it. Prevent it.

Rob: Me?

Rose: You, Rob. You must tell him to call it off. You know Dave; he thinks he's doing it for you.

But Rob turned again to the window and started again to trace his curlicues.

'No, Rose. I've had enough. Let happen happen. Let it all happen.'

[A version of this story was first published as P. Clough (1999) Crises of schooling and the 'crisis of representation': the story of Rob, *Qualitative Inquiry*, 5(3): 428–48.]

6 | Bev

Listen to this. It's a sort of poem:

> There is shit everywhere. Because he has tried to reach the bathroom there is shit in a trail across the carpet and – though she does not find this for several days – there is shit on a pile of folded curtains by the top of the stairs.

> There is a way of dealing with this shit; one thing is not to rub it into the carpet, but to pull what can be pulled with a cloth onto damp paper tissue and then to tamp towels hard down, pressing hard down as on dough. This takes ten or twelve minutes.

> Matthew is wedged on the toilet; his shoulder is fallen hard against the wall so that his bottom is wedged in the ring of the toilet seat. When Bev finishes the floor he is sleeping and he starts slightly as she touches his arm. She lifts him and puts his arm around her shoulder. There is nothing in the toilet bowl.

> In her bed she arranges his bald head cradled in her armpit and when he turns slightly some minutes later his mouth takes her nipple through her nightdress.

> It is 4.30 and there is no sound outside. At 5.10 a car can be heard some streets away and some minutes later the first bird starts. At 6.20 Bev turns off the alarm clock before it can start to ring.

Not that many years ago I watched a woman fall apart in a school. The school was falling apart, too, and I knew – without being able to name it at the time – that there was some connection between these disintegrations. The school recovered.

I was working as a researcher, and I'd been studying how schools dealt with kids with learning difficulties. Someone said: 'Oh, you should go to Whatsitsname Comprehensive, that's *very* interesting . . .'

I phoned the headteacher and was there within two days. It was clear I was welcome: yes, they would be happy for me to visit the school. I could talk to as many of the staff as I wished, and in return I should do a 'sketch' for them. 'It's timely. It will do us some good,' said the head. 'You can hold a mirror up to us. We run a good ship but it will do us good to see ourselves more clearly. We're in something of a Cretacean period' *(whatever that meant)*.

I didn't like him. Miles was young for the job – 40, 43, maybe – and had a clearly expensive suit. He was tall and bald and his body was obviously trained firm beneath his shirt without jacket. At the time I thought that men like this should not be headteachers of schools in Labour-controlled authorities. Waiting also in his office was Bev, head of the special needs department. Bev weighed – when I met her – some 22 stones, and was maybe 5 foot 6. I learned as a fact later – though I could sense at the time – that she smoked 40 cigarettes a day (which is quite an achievement on a full timetable); certainly in all the time I knew her she seemed short of a decent breath. She walked always with some difficulty – as if she suffered some continual agony – something which was apart from the weight-given gait.

Miles: Bev will show you round – Bev is my right-hand man, aren't you, darling?

Bev: There you go – all talk no action. What about my extra 0.5 teacher, then?

M: Bev and I go back a long way, don't we? We've had some fights . . . We have that . . .

B: . . . but we come out of them, don't we, darling?

M: When I come round to your point of view we do! Don't believe her – it's Bev runs this show; I'm just a suit in committee.

I was embarrassed for – as on a stage in front of me – they were quite clearly nibbling and nipping at each other beneath the banter, the banter oddly freighted with a sexuality. They contrasted so much, Miles spare and tall and somehow his very baldness was vigorous; Bev quite round and flushed and looking hard for breath. And he was at once her son, her lover and her boss; and Bev, too, played.

I couldn't name this sexuality at the time; I didn't know the name of my embarrassment until – in fact – I had written '*There is shit everywhere* . . .' Bev took me to the staff coffee-room and then to a small room off it, set aside for smokers. We smoked together.

'He's all right is Miles, I can handle Miles. We've had our ding-dongs but we know where we stand. He's given me a lot of head – he's given me a lot of stick, too – but we're all right. But that's Miles – if you show him what you can do he's behind you all the way.'

We smoked again – cigarettes end-on – and I learned the first somethings of her life: she was single, 51, she was Irish, she had diabetes, she lived with her Dad. This was a list – a sort of summary – which gave up no hint of difficulty. Later I would understand something of what held this list together. I talked about my study.

> B: Well in some ways you couldn't have come at a better time; we're sort of in crisis – did Miles tell you? – well not crisis but – how shall I say? – in a melting pot. Miles's a bugger but I love him – he's thrown up this plan where we remake my department – he does this, I think, when he's bored; like, throws in a little grenade just to see what will happen. He's a rascal, he's infuriating but he's generally right, the bugger.

I talked with Bev for an hour that day, and again two days later. She gave me a history of the department, and it was then she started to tell me how this history was involved with her own. *'My dad became really sick that year and I had to take some time off.'* But she did not speak further of him on this occasion, nor actually ever properly. This life and its sadness she hardly spoke of, as though I knew it all and so in the end, by another route, I did.

When we met the third time, we talked for nearly two hours of Bev's life as a child in Dublin, a student in Liverpool, as houseparent in a remand centre, teaching in Africa, then social work here and there, and finally teaching here. And on this occasion, I remember a moment when she took her cigarette to her mouth, and as rapidly pulled her hand away again, and said: *'Christ I stink of shit.'* I laughed and she said, *'I was up half the night, Dad's incontinent now.'*

And from this time I think I started to feel Matthew – the dying Matthew – watching.

Elsewhere – out of the immediate compass of Bev's life, that is – elsewhere, things were no better, possibly worse. In the fourth and last week of my visits, I was met by the school secretary, who said that Miles, the head, would see me at 10.30. It was clear that this was not an invitation as such. He had a simple point to make, which you can hear being driven home in the tape-recording of our brief conversation. It goes something like:

Miles: Bev is poorly.
PC: Oh? Er . . .
M: Bev is sick; very, very sick.
PC: I know that she . . .
M: And has been for a long time, for some long time actually.
PC: I know her Dad's ill, I . . .
M: But short of actually forbidding her to come to work there's not much I can do, well that's not true, I did, I did forbid her one week because she's no use to anyone – to anyone – in this state.

Miles asked me for my report, the 'sketch' I had promised.

PC: It'll take a week or two to polish, but . . .
M: Yes, but the gist. What d'you think of us? Of Bev's department?

What did I think of Bev's department? It was in chaos. It was falling apart and had become as friable as its head of department. Few structures held the thing together, beyond those which organized Bev's own spirit. To be sure, there were timetables, a policy of sorts, schedules for staff to refer children for help. But these things were contingent, mere stuff that routed Bev's energy. My hunch was that when Bev was vigorous, the whole show thrived, was large with her presence and verve. But when Bev began to fall apart – as her dying Dad suffered on and on – the department, too, sagged. So: lessons were missed, or started late; departmental meetings were cancelled without warning; vital case conferences were ill prepared. These were the things to point to later in the account when the infection of the department needed a name in a report. But what really happened was a matter in the nerves. For Bev sat the while holding court among the dozen or so smokers who had been granted a separate staff room. A 15-minute break mid-morning is just long enough for two, sometimes three cigarettes end-on if you leave your lesson sharp enough on the bell, and will always be a few minutes late for the class at 11. If you really have to see Bev you must find her in this smoky room. And I had met Ken, the second in the department, whom I knew had adored Bev; who indeed had come to the school just so as to work with Bev; but whose love is exhausted.

'I couldn't *start* to tell you,' Ken said. 'I couldn't *start* . . . this for starters.'

And he held up a file pinched at the corner between his thumb and forefinger,

'This is a . . . a child . . . a . . . some *scrap* waiting desperately but *desperately* for a statement so he can have a support assistant, yeh? And where's the file and where's it been for the last five – *five* – months? *I'll* tell you where it's been for five months: under Bev's fat arse in the smokers'!'

And – indeed – it seemed it had been under the crocheted red cushion of Bev's armchair. Ken's hair is sticking with sweat close to his head and his shirt is very wet around the armpits. Actually he is very close to tears. From the way he is holding the file, you could think that it was soiled.

And every time we walked from smokers' to classroom, children quite swarmed about Bev.

'Eh Miss! Miss, me Dad's out on Friday – Miss! Miss! Look at me trainers! – Miss will yer tell 'im? Will yer miss? I aren't goin' to no bloody doctor – Miss.'

But I had also seen her moving like a mayoress or a ship down the corridors, dealing out a word of warmth or counsel here, a cuff or a warning finger there. For all the world like some benign potentate entering court fat with bounty and swarming with plaintiffs. And I once saw her lead a boy – a young man, some six or eight inches bigger than her – I saw her lead this youth squealing by his ear the length of a corridor. We were passing him bent in menace over another boy – 'bring it tomorrow Paki or tha' dees . . .' – and she led him squealing to her office.

'Ah! Gerroff! Bloody gerroff! Tha'rt bloody 'urtin' me!'

'I'll hurt yer, Derek Turner.'

'Ah'll 'ave police on thee, whalearse, our kid'll pop thee! Ow! Fuckin' gerroff!'

Once in her office, safe from other eyes, the boy's curses became tears, and Bev held him on her bosom.

'Yer a great daft thing, Derek Turner, what are you?'

'Gret . . . [sob] . . . daft . . . [sob] . . . thing, miss.'

So . . . the gist, Miles? The gist is a larger than life, smaller than life woman who made magic and chaos around her; loved children, lost files; breathed smiles into hopeless scraps; knew it was hopeless to try to teach Susan Elsworth to read just yet, so taught her to sew; sat on Ahmed Birham's doorstep until his father opened the door nearly two February hours later and just had to let her in; forgot to attend two tribunals, and brought the wrong notes to a third; neglected her body – abused it with excess of nicotine and sweet foods and sometimes alcohol and starved it of the routine health checks and daily blood tests and injections it needed to maintain some sort of existence. She ignored her own illness in the witness of her father's – doing just enough to keep going for another day – and another – and another – and another. What, Miles? This is sentimental? If it is, Miles, so be it.

Of course I didn't give Miles a report. I didn't need to, and he knew I wouldn't. And I only heard what happened to Bev some 15 months later, when I met one of the teachers on holiday in Filey. Bev's Dad had died 6 weeks after I'd finished at the school. Bev had sold the house where they'd lived and moved to a modern flat – a-nice-neat-fresh-smelling-flat-for-one. Things at school had not improved, though Bev had by now exhausted the patience – the love, possibly – of everyone but the kids, who still mobbed her. Then a preliminary report by government inspectors found Special Needs wanting, and Miles got his licence to act as he had always wanted. He sent for her and suggested some leave; she refused, but he told her to go home and take a couple of weeks, really get over her father. Miles, I was told, 'explained' his long-held concern for Bev at the next routine staff meeting. How he had worried about her health for some time – how he had insisted that she take time to recuperate.

I did not need to be at the meeting to know what happened. I had spent a month in the school; I knew Miles, the staff and their confusion of respect and disgust for Bev.

Neither was I there the day Bev left, of course, but I was told of how the bloated and gasping Bev was taken home that day; sent home, actually, by taxi, though Miles would have had an arm around her as she left by the back. And I have an image of her leaving Miles's office all puffed up with tears, all florid and a tiny forbearing smile slightly softening the rictus of her terror.

It is of course a fantastic indictment of us all that Bev's body – Bev's severely reduced body, Bev now livid and finally rigorous – was not found until 11 days after this day. Her new neighbours didn't know her, she bought milk from the supermarket, had no routine callers. Oddly, she was discovered by a burglar who decently called the police (though – for she pungently had no further need of it – relieved Bev of her purse as his fee). It seems that in her anxiety she had forgotten to eat, or else had not eaten properly. Also she had fallen – a gash to her head had bled on to the carpet. Her ulcerous legs had borne the brunt of her illness. There could only be an open verdict. But – the teacher told me – there was enough cat food out for 10 days, maybe 2 weeks.

I don't know what the real conclusion to this story is, for it's not a story simply exhausted by Bev's death. But with the passage of time the story has assembled itself from a clutch of data and – nude of any critical clothes – is simple enough. What is left when the data – the given – are returned to their owners is something simple and terrible; something grave and constant in human suffering. And schooling, it seems to me, is all but theorized by Bev's body.

[A version of this story was first published as P. Clough (2001) Bev: an embodied theory of schooling? *Auto/Biography* (Journal of the British Sociological Association Auto/Biography Study Group), IX(1): 123–5.]

7 | Lolly: the final word

You pull on a thread and little suspect how the whole weave puckers.

In 1998 I plucked a thread from the weave of lives I was then interested in. On Thursday 22 February 2001, the chickens came home, not in search of a quiet perch but wild-eyed, the-worm-turned, and full of wrath.

I know it was 8 p.m. because the game started just as the door was knocked. I'd been working in the front room, in what I used as a study, right up till the match started. There were piles of books around, and I was deeply irritated that someone should be at the door at this time.

I heard Philip, my son, go to the door, could just hear him say 'Hang on . . .' or some such, and then – of an instant – a man whom I had never seen before stood large in the door to my front room. I knew him immediately.

I knew him immediately and immediately situated my guilt before him.

'*Doctor* Clough,' he said and there were scare-quotes hung with bane around the word, like it was a turd in his mouth.

'*Doctor* Clough.'

'Lol. Lolly,' I said.

Three, maybe four years before, I had written a story about this man's younger brother, a boy I had met when I worked as a researcher looking at a big inner-city school. The boy was nicknamed Molly, an abbreviation of Molinetti. His family had come to England from Milan shortly after the Second World War and made a decent life and living out of ice cream. But Molly was a Bad Lad, which was what drew me to him. He was of course a good lad, which was perhaps what drew me more.

I had told this story in a book I wrote. I wrote about a boy lost in a school, a big school, fairly downtown in this big, Northern city tired with industrial collapse; a city fitfully tense with a substantial Pakistani community, brought indifferently so many years before thousands of miles.

I told the story of a boy struggling to make a mark within a school which was itself struggling somewhere at the ragged ends of Whitehall policies – a school living on subsistence funding; trying honestly to do right by its kids; to respect – to celebrate, even – its majority, second-generation immigrant community; the backs of the teachers, meanwhile, stabbed by successive swingeing government scorns . . .

And in the middle of all this, a local lad.

Well: local, as in 'not Asian', but no more local than many of those; local as one who had lived all his 15 years in that city, and who spoke local. But European-white. And the real locus for Molly was a dense brew of brutally received machismo and deep currents of racial jostling; a filial desire to please, a school struggling with political correctness, and the whole wired with the quirky explosive spurts of testosterone. And I was there when he and the school decided they'd had enough of each other, when Molly struck a teacher and his schooling came to an end. Two years later his life did too, when he died joy-riding with kids a few years younger. I'd written most of this – and more – in my story.

And here was Lorenzo – Lol, his brother – whom Molly had told me about. Molly's mum had had Lol when she was 15. Some 17 years later – when she was 32 – she had Molly himself, no others in between. The man in front of me was about 40, probably actually short but he seemed – from my rooted place down in an armchair – big, menacing and in fact the fire threw his large shadow on the wall behind him.

'*Doctor* Clough,' he said.

'Lol. Lolly,' I said.

I knew him immediately and immediately situated myself before him, somehow cowering. Whatever animal response to a large stranger suddenly in the nest was fled. Philip had followed him, and was concerned.

'It's all right, Phil,' I said. 'It's all right' (though I could hear how the smallest warble in my voice said otherwise).

Phil said nothing but left the room. Lol remained standing, and I had a sense that it would be impertinent to invite him to sit. I made to stand, but he raised a finger – just the finger – slightly with incredibly powerful economy of movement.

We were both silent, while Lol appraised the room.

'So: this is where it is, where it all happens.'

'I don't know . . .' I started.

'Where children are killed. Where families are . . . what? Displayed like circus freaks?'

He went to the window.

'I wouldn't have taken you for an Ink Spots man.'

'Sorry?'

He was standing by the window, and had picked up a CD case from a pile of half a dozen on the coffee table.

'Glenn Miller. Count Basie.'

'They're my Dad's. Were my Dad's, they . . .'

They were part of what little remained of 78 years, sifted – after the second-hand dealers had left – into a single black bin-liner, all else shovelled into the big industrial waste containers at the back of the nursing home. With such speed a life dematerializes.

But Lolly wasn't listening; he was grazing along the bookshelves, and we both knew what he was looking for. But he was delaying the moment of finding, or maybe just actually interested in the mixed messages set up by my own 50-year accumulation of words.

'What's this? A directory?'

He was holding out my old, flaking teaching copy of *Adolescent Boys of East London*.

'No, it's . . .'

'I *know* what it is *Dr* Clough, I *know*. It's a *joke*, see?'

'I'm sorry, I didn't . . .'

'You didn't know I'd know such a thing, right?'

'No, it's just . . . that.'

But, again, he had turned back to the shelves as though the audience was over, and was again busy with his curious librarianship. Then he found the book, the book I had written with the story of his little brother. He opened it as though he knew exactly where to find the story, and tossed it in my lap. I had still barely looked up since he entered.

'Read it. No. Out loud. Fucking *speak* it.'

I started.

'There is no clear window into the inner life of a person . . .'

'No. The next page. Here give it to me. This bit.'

and his finger pushed the passage in front of me:

'Read this, this bit.'

It was a passage which quoted – more or less word for word – the first meeting I had had with Molly's – with Lolly's – mother, and the first words she'd said to me I started to read.

'*What . . . er, what should I do/what er . . .*'

'That's not what it says. Read what's on the page. *Read it!*'

The words on the page said: *Wha' ah do, eh? Eh? Ah buy 'im a bice an' wha' 'e do, eh? 'E sell 'e!* In the account, my story, Molly's mum had bought him a bicycle, and Molly had quickly sold it. I was silent.

'Go on. Read it. Fucking read it. *Now.*'

Lol's finger was back in my face.

'I . . .'

'READ IT. Just-fucking-just-read-it.'

But I was crying, and Lol turned away to the window and himself started to read out loud the account with even more Hollywood caricature than even I had loaded it with.

'Wha' you goin' do wi' 'im, eh? 'E goes a Youth club in a new trouse, 'e comes 'ome in a jean is not 'is, eh? So where you trouse, eh? I say 'im: Franny where you trouse, eh? An' 'e say: "ah doornt naw mam . . ." '

He paused.

'Do you have a mother, *Doctor* Clough?'

I nodded, snivelling now.
'Hm,' he nodded at me, and turning back to the page started to read again from my account:

'When I visit Molly's home to meet his mother, I am amused by the identical downy moustache that they share.'

Again he paused, maybe some 10 seconds.

'Does *your* mother have a moustache, *Doctor* Clough?'

I was silent, immobile, not sure whether it was a real question or not.

'I said: does *your* mother have a moustache, *Doctor* Clough?'

I tried to say, I muttered: 'No.'

'Speak up! Say it – say "No, my mother doesn't have a moustache." '

Punctuated with deep snorts of snot and tears, I managed to say

'No, my mother doesn't have a moustache.'

'Of *course* she doesn't, *Doctor* Clough,' he laughed loud. 'Of *course* she doesn't!'

But then in an instant was solemn again.

'That was *my* mother, *Doctor* Clough. And that was *my* brother.'

He was stood at the window, tracing elaborate little curls on the condensation, and I noticed for the first time that the television was still full on, and the match was stopped while a player, clearly badly hurt, twitched and writhed as assistants tried to calm him.

Lol seemed to be talking to the window, so quietly I could barely hear him.

'What were you doing? What did you want? Eh? What did you want from my brother? 'Cos you certainly got it. A rich story, was it? A rich piece of research? How your audiences must have loved those tales!'

He turned from the window and faced into the room.

'You killed that boy. Mm? Do you think he'd have been pissing about like that if he hadn't had you for an audience? D'you think so? D'you think he'd have punched that teacher? Do you think he'd have been expelled if you hadn't . . . if you hadn't been there? If you hadn't written the script for him? Eh?'

Lol was silent now for maybe as much as two minutes. I started several times to say something, but each time could find no words. Finally I managed to say, in a sort of tearful whisper:

'Look. Can we sort this out? Can we . . .'

Lol was still stood against the window, silent, looking out on the silent street. He raised an indifferent finger to the window and drew a line indifferently across the scars of earlier sketches on the condensation. When he turned, I was little with fear in my chair.

'What d'you want? What can I do? Say, Lol – what d'you want?'

In the back room I heard the phone ring three times and then Phil's voice a room away, faintly.

'Lol, please.'

Lol stayed with his back to the window, quite motionless.

'Lol, what do you want?'

And then he moved slowly across the room till he stood above me, looking down.

'Nothing,' he said finally. 'Nothing.'

The door opened and as Phil made to come in, I tried to stand. Phil made to speak, but was arrested by what he saw, mouth quite open: Lol towering above me, me trying to stand, a patch of wet across my groin and down to one knee.

'Nothing. Or perhaps . . .'

and he spread his hands to take in me, Phil, the room and all:

'Or perhaps this.'

And was gone. I am done with stories.

[An earlier version of this story appeared as P. Clough (2002) Theft and ethics in life portrayal: the final word, *International Journal of Qualitative Studies in Education.*]

8 | Hard to tell: reading the stories

Quelqu'un pourrait dire de moi que j'ai seulement fait ici un amas de
fleurs etrangeres, n'y ayant fourni du mien que le filet a les lier . . .[1]

(Montaigne 1580)

Introduction

What do the stories in this book have to say about educational settings?
How do they relate to other forms of educational research and report? What
can other students of educational research learn from them?

The concepts that are entailed in these questions – of morality, methodology and pedagogy, and their essential unity in ethical practice – inform
the remainder of the book. This remainder has two parts. In the first – this
chapter – I bring together some notes on the eventual provenance of the
stories with my reflections on what they currently signify for me as expressions of critical inquiry. The chapter is thus effectively a set of critical foot-
notes.

The stories in the previous chapters are all curious things to evaluate.
How should they be evaluated? What criteria should be used? These rather
dry questions are important considerations within the ethnographic context.
What follows here, therefore, are five 'readings'. They are my own glosses
on the stories and they uncover first the sources and contexts of the stories
and second my discovery within those stories, what *I* find in them. Each
reading begins with the reiteration of the opening and closing lines of its
story.

A reading of Klaus

> I've met my father and his sons in so many special schools.
> A man I was really frightened of was a miner from Bresswell; he had
> served in the post-war army, mainly in Germany, and named his son
> Klaus in honour and memory, I presume, of a greater life, culture and
> identity than he enjoyed in this bleak mining village. He had a
> bayonet over the fireplace. His wife – the mother – had left years
> before and he had brought Klaus up largely alone with some help
> from his nearby mother. He was in all respects what would be called,
> I think, 'a man's man'.
>
> * * *
>
> Watching him go off up the lane for the bus, his only son left in this
> school for damaged boys. Poor man; he must himself have been
> fighting some vestige of memory of love and warmth; and must be
> damaged so much; and must like me not know who he is when it
> comes to love. Certain postures, certain roles we can manage – a
> man, a lecturer, a miner – we can do these things inside a certain
> identity which comes with them; but inside love, where you're really
> on your own, where love's own dynamism and structure should hold
> and guide and lead, oh no, we are beggars, opportunists, scavengers,
> tricksters: because love's own rules – love's spontaneous, natural
> rules, love's intuitive rules – were taken out, beaten out of us, and in
> their place were put other rules: guilt, fear, recrimination.
>
> And tricks of silence, exile and cunning.

Sources and contexts

The story arose from a 'real' enough task, which was to write something of
the experience of a number of boys assessed as having behavioural difficulties in a school, where I was researching teachers' perspectives on learning difficulty. The report was duly written, and relates the phenomena of
disaffected and disturbing behaviours both to the structure of the school's
management and to the detail of then current national policy concerns. But
the story of *Klaus* does not have that sort of reality.

The work involved interviewing teachers and students as well as 'hangin''
around' with various groups of (mainly) boys (who feature large in *Molly*).
In the final report, their cut-and-paste testimony illustrates a fairly simple
argument about the causal relationship between school structures and
student behaviours. But though such thoughts must have attended at some
level as I gathered the data, it was the curious mixture of ease and unease of

mixing with the boys which really occupied me as I set to writing my report. The boys unnerved and irritated my role as researcher, though it was only later – through writing what I then called 'Again fathers and sons' – that I realized how infected was this role with my own experiences as a child, a (relatively disaffected) student, and more recently a father. The boy in the story – Klaus – strayed into my research as I learned something of the family relationships of these other boys and as, I realized, I started to see some fossils in my own experience.

Klaus was a 9-year-old boy with moderate learning difficulties, and emotional and behavioural difficulties (or 'educationally subnormal' and 'maladjusted' as he might then have technically been identified in UK legislation) which had already seen him excluded from two schools; I met him when – in the late 1970s – I had started work in the short-term residential unit where he had been placed. I had 'forgotten' Klaus until then, I suppose because the memory of my dealings with him and his father was uncomfortable.

Of the 'facts', I should record that this boy and his father 'existed' as they do in the story; my visit to the house and the father's visit to the school 'happened' in precisely the way that my memory reconstructs them in the story. In this sense, there is no *material* import to the story. But its data have no formal record, and its particular structure is achieved through a working out of a very personal agenda and it is verified only in collision with the experience of the reader.

What do I find in the story?

I want here to discuss the embedded issues of research and the mutual construction of self and story. In these respects, *Klaus* brings together a number of themes: the role of the researcher's own experience in reporting that of others; the capacity of narrative methods in the social sciences to report human experience; and the virtue of the 'self'-consciously fictional story as a form which can bring and hold together the experiences of the researcher and of the 'subject'. These themes are the inevitable warp and weft of the book and so occur and recur. They are demonstrated in the stories and are centres of experience in these readings, but *Klaus* insists upon particular discussion of research and self and the mutual constructions of self and story, so I shall take some space here to unpack those two.

Research and self

'I've met my father and his sons in so many special schools'
The role of the researcher's self in the construction of research accounts is a ground being cleared in the increasing occupation of educational research with

the insertion of the researcher themself in the process of research. Reflections on research collected, for example, by Walford (1991), Vulliamy and Webb (1992) and Clough and Barton (1995) emphasize not only the growing critical, but also the reflexive self-awareness of educational inquiry, and in the introductions to each of these collections is seen the impulse to such revelation located and justified in a particular tradition of human science study. An example of this sort of approach may be found in Clough and Barton (1995), where we asked various researchers in the field of SEN/disability to review a particular study of theirs in the light of these (among other) questions:

- What assumptions about SEN/disability do I have which are inevitably present in the way I conceive of the study?
- Why and how did these assumptions suggest or require the particular methods, which I chose?
- What assumptions about 'how the world operates' are given with these methods?
- In what ways am I changed by the research?

The responses are naturally various, but all the accounts set out to explore the constructions of SEN/disability at work in the given project, understand the dilemmas and insights involved in the research and – above all – show something of the engagement of the researcher in the work.

Klaus and I are central to the story but it is my own identity which lies at the heart of the meaning constructed through this story as a kind of 'testament' (Hutton-Jarvis 1999).

> I can see myself standing there in my blue Harris Tweed jacket and saying 'It's Mr Clough. Mr Clough from the school.' Try it: there are not many ways to say those words and even fewer meanings.

My own identity as I constructed it in relation to my own father is central too – stripped as I was of power and confidence in the presence of this other father:

> I was in an instant frightened; I knew I had strayed across some tracks and I was frightened – not by the man, but by the power singing around me. I had no language here, no voice, and without language no power.

> The fear that day was a simple animal fear and it was a galvanic nothing – mere animal twitch – by the other fear that I later felt in front of Klaus's father. I was immobilized by that other fear. That was something that reached down the canal of my composure and found the ever-leaking corrosion of my father's presence.

But narrative and the expectations of narrative make a problem for those who seek to write 'believable' stories. For in making 'plausible' narrative I (we) are sometimes forced (tempted) into creating characters who deny the totality of human experienced. 'Believable' characters are often dangerously insubstantial, bearing only a trace of the realities of life *as lived* by some realities. Fictional characters – if they are to be believed – are often *capable* of bearing only a certain portion of pain, of horror. For harrowing experiences that seem disproportionate to what it is 'reasonable' to expect of any single human being dis/locate our own construction of human experience as we *expect* it to be. It can be implausible to create – in story – a character who bears, simultaneously, all the stresses of life, yet such lives are lived. Were I to try to present such chaos of experience in a single character I would (should?) be accused of giving the character too much pain – overloading the situation – creating an implausible (larger than life) experience for one person to carry – dis/connecting with reality. Yet such *is* the reality of some human experience. How might I, for example, write a (true) story of a woman whose life is fraught with pain, illness and mental suffering and how, in so doing might I avoid the accusation of painting an impossibly catastrophic picture – of pushing the pain too far – of sensationalizing? Of narrative we often *require* some element of silver lining – however tarnished and remote it might be. Life and its portions of agony, injustice, fear and illness does not always so oblige, and narrative which portrays such rawness may well attract criticism because it is too dark.

There are new maps to draw in the making of 'fictional' characters, maps to help us in the task of writing *people* in narrative. Translating life's realities *as lived* by men and women into story, and doing in such a way as still to be believed, is *the* ethnographic challenge.

Mutual constructions

Interviewee behaviour inevitably reveals patterns created in the mind in another time; life-historical study is therefore driven by a sort of search for fossils – in the texts constructed in interview – which give a sense and an index of those other times. It is the researcher's task, then, to trace how those other times lead in the instance of this or that subject to the very present constitution of a self and of the set of practices which define it.

I am concerned, through story, to rattle the bars which I see any given social science methods as throwing up around attempts to characterize experience. Even life-historical method – by virtue of being a method – may subvert the profound human impulse to tell stories – stories driven by symbols rather than 'data'. We need to look more closely at the narratives which organize *our own* experience and not allow them to be subverted by the method which we customarily use. For despite the sterility of instruments, we never come innocent to a research task, or a situation of events; rather we situate these events not merely in the institutional meanings which our profession provides, but also constitute them as expressions of ourselves.

A reading of Molly

> Tim Booth asked me: *How do you give a voice to people who lack words?*
>
> My problem with Molly is not that he *lacks* words, but rather that they can spill out of him with a wild, fairground pulse; they are sparklers, he waves them splashing around him. And my other problem with Molly's words is that many of them are not very nice; they are squibs that make you jump out of the way. For the moment I think that these are my only problems.
>
> * * *
>
> At the hospital the police were keen to take statements but Mark and the women were silent and would say nothing; the police were formally polite at first and finally – convinced that Mark knew but was protecting his attacker – derisive. They threw the fag and his dykes out at 3.40 a.m.

Sources and contexts

Molly is an attempt to dispose empirical data as a persuasive art which challenges some common notions of voice and of learning difficulty. But such an attempt to articulate in this way is not without difficulty.

This is a story of boys, teachers and a school with difficulties. It is a story used to express the difficulties of articulating difficulties, and the difficulties of those who are *differently articulate*. The chapter is built around a story which I put together five years after my involvement with a school which was of great interest: a big (about 2000 students) place fairly downtown in a big city tired with industrial collapse; fitfully tense – in this retrenchment – with a substantial Pakistani community brought so many years ago thousands of miles indifferently as so many operatives; and made slightly famous by local politicians who polarized each other into caricatures of left and right (one Labour councillor described the Tory leader – in his presence – as *'itler wi' knobs on*; this without a smile (Clough 1995: 132).

My broad project to understand the culture of 'special' education in that school is described in Clough and Barton (1995), but this particular story is knit from my more specific attempts in that school to get a handle on the 'bad lads', where resistance – being bad – called for some flair on the part of white lads in a school 94 per cent populated by Asian – and a handful of African Caribbean – kids.

What I find in the story

The story is an amalgam of raw transcribed observation, interview events, notes of conversations, my own research journal and imports of my own knowing and belief. The story is slightly knit with what Yalom (1991: ix) calls *'symbolically equivalent substitutes'* to be sure of anonymity. In the case of this particular story, I owe something – though I'm not quite sure what – to George Riseborough (1993) for his 'GBH: the Gobbo Barmy Harmy', which is one of the most shocking things I've ever read. Riseborough's ethnographic study of a group of Youth Training Scheme adolescents is an incredible achievement, but horrid.

There are horrid things in this story, too; difficult to write and difficult to read. But I believe they only narrowly disguise more truly horrid things. There are in this story many of the difficulties of inequality which pervade much of education, and which are especially entangled in any discussion of children with difficulties. The story is fraught with issues of endemic racism bound up with clashes of culture and struggles of the working class and unemployed. Young people – born British – are still maligned for their origins, and their abilities to speak two (or more) languages either go unnoticed or – worse – are a source of ridicule. For me, racism is a key theme of the story, yet another reader, bringing to the story a different life experience, may well say that the theme has more to do with sexuality than with race (see Nayak and Kehily 1996).

And this is a story mainly about boys, the kinds of boys who, in the 1990s when the story was set, made up the one in twelve who leave school with no General Certificate of Secondary Education (GCSE) passes (Department for Education and Employment (DfEE 1997a: 79). They are boys who have not achieved what school wanted of them; boys who might not have known what they wanted of themselves; and boys who could or would not achieve what their families wanted of them (Skelton 1996). In 1996, 48 per cent of 14-year-old boys scored level 5 or above on National Curriculum tests; for girls the figure was 66 per cent, (DfEE 1997a). Boys' underachievement in English set alarm bells ringing again (Wiltshire 1996; Frater 1997; School Curriculum and Assessment Authority (SCAA) 1997). Low achievement in literacy inhibits a great deal of the curriculum, and pupils may well experience struggle in each aspect of the curriculum. In 1997 and 1998 national strategies were put in place to address issues of underachievement (DfEE 1998). A Government White Paper on Education (DfEE 1997a) *Excellence in Schools*, closely followed by a Green Paper (DfEE 1997b), set the tone for consultation on future government policy on special educational needs. The White Paper stated:

> Education is the key to creating a society which is dynamic and productive, offering opportunity and fairness to all. It is the Government's

top priority. We will work in partnership with all those who share our passion and sense of urgency for higher standards.

(DfEE 1997a: 9)

For the boys in this story – and for Molly especially – there was no such opportunity, no such 'fairness'; only blame and expectation of continued and increasingly complex difficulties, and perpetual undesirable behaviour (Mahony 1985). There was passion but it was not a passion for lessons or learning; it was a passion driven by survival.

Some inhibited voices and the impasse of policy

Voice does not itself struggle for rights, but is disposed after rights are established; voice is licensed by these rights. It follows from this view that the task for research is largely one of 'turning up the volume' on the depressed or inaudible voice; this is achieved primarily through a series of policy and legislative modulations, though also by means of various technico-legal interventions thus licensed (see particularly Glaser and Strauss 1967).

But in fact, listening to subjects with special educational needs throws into a particular relief all the generically difficult issues of researching 'voice' – issues to do with who is listening to whom, why and – above all, perhaps – in whose interests? For, like most research subjects in the majority of studies, they are identified because they reflect – if not quite represent – a particular population; they represent the experiences of a more or less distinct category (black males, newly qualified teachers, Year 8 girls, and so on); thus by definition, subjects with special educational needs are identified because they are categorically different (if not deficient). In such research they are primarily interesting, therefore, because of a perceived difference – however benignly understood, and however politically motivated the study (Davie et al. 1996).

Finding a language for working through these hunches is difficult. *Molly* is – rather like Burgess's *A Clockwork Orange* – at once 'a work too didactic to be artistic' and 'art dragged into the arena of morality' (Morrison 1996). But as a 'reflexive project of the self' (Giddens 1991) it perhaps casts some light. People who have responded to the story say that it depicts many struggles; the struggles of characters looking in different directions, where sometimes gazes collide, suffering intermittently from periods of seeming blindness. The researcher – they say – battles to locate himself in his relationship with his subjects. The teachers make stabbing attempts at negotiating a discourse with each other and their pupils. The boys spar among themselves, vying for macho supremacy and wit, against a background of familial brutishness. It is a tragic soap opera which brings together so many discordant voices in a chorus of protest about the impossible roles that society situates them to play. The actors struggle with each other, use scripts from different plays, sometimes communicating, sometimes not.

The research act of listening to voice must always involve the (broadly defined) processes of both mediation and translation (Tierney 1995); and these functions may be particularly indicated where there are doubts about the capacity of the subject to express an intention; doubts, that is, about their powers of articulation. This is, of course, a function of a much larger question of the power relations between the researcher and the researched (Dyson 1998).

For the most part, life stories are articulated by the conventionally articulate (see Booth 1996 for an extended discussion and bibliography). How is such advocacy justified, and at what cost? Sparkes (1994), for example, justifies such acts of writing – by people who hold advantaged positions – in terms of their more effective challenge to their privileged peers *by virtue of those positions*; he argues that studies by marginalized individuals or groups may reflect false consciousness, or may be 'coated with self-protective ideology'. More pragmatically, Sparkes questions whether – almost by definition – the marginalized individual possesses the resources (of various cultural capital) for effectively telling their own story.

For some writers, the project is thus an attempt to forge dialogical empathies between the alienated, between each of our 'othernesses' (see, for example, Rorty 1989). Thus Geertz seeks to enlarge

> the possibility of intelligible discourse between people quite different from one another in interest, outlook, wealth and power, and yet contained in a world where, tumbled as they are into endless connection, it is increasingly difficult to get out of each other's way.
>
> (Geertz 1988: 147)

But this essentially humanist (Barone 1998) project of solidarity and empathy is not enough for some story writers (and readers), who act politically through 'storied' voice specifically to emancipate; who ultimately seek, that is, a redistribution of power. Thus the search is for the articulation of a persuasive voice which will challenge readers' interests, privileges and prejudices. As bell hooks (1991) has it, such writers can provide searing, harrowing 'chronicles of pain' – though she reminds us that these may well serve merely to 'keep in place existing structures of domination' (hooks 1991: 59) if they do not bring about a deep unease in the reader.

It is my experience that *Molly* certainly brings about unease, and effectively dramatizes – without didacticism – the subtleties of power relations which are tacitly at its centre.

A reading of Rob

When Rob Joynson was 43 he came into school on a Tuesday morning much as usual; and passing at 10.40 by a maths class taken by Michelle G. – a probationer of 23 – and hearing terrible noise; and seeing through the window a boy at the back fetch a fat gob on Michelle's back as she walked down the aisle smiling, smiling too, too nervously, her hands doing 'Down, please: down, down' at the noise; seeing this marbled yellow gob on Michelle's ordinary blouse on her decent body, Rob Joynson rushed into the room and to the back and took the boy – Mark something – by the ears, both ears, and pulled him up out of – through almost – his desk and repeatedly smashed his head against a chart of tessellations on the wall. And Michelle pulled at him from behind and screamed, and he twisted the boy down by his ears and pushed at him with his foot, kicking until he was quite under the desk. Then Rob started to cry and there was terrible silence – where there had been terrible noise – but for Rob searching for breath to fuel the small fearful wails which broke from him. When – thank God – someone laughed finally, unable to stay with the pain a moment longer, Rob fled the room.

* * *

As much as two full minutes later, Rose stirred.

'I must go.'

Rob didn't move. In the dark room it was impossible to see whether he was looking in or out the room.

'There's one more thing, Rob.'

But then Rob obviously turned, so he was facing in the room.

Rob: Can there be? Don't tell me: I'm to have my balls chopped off in assembly.

Rose: Don't joke, Rob. Listen. Dave Bird is planning action.

Rob: Action?

Rose: Unofficial strike, tomorrow. I think he'll get half, maybe two-thirds of the staff. Anyway, enough to have press, TV and everyone down here. Then everyone loses everything: you, Mark, the school, the authority – it'll all go up. Do you follow me? It will be open, national, bloody warfare. You will be a national figure, Rob. The *Sun* will be published from your doorstep. You must stop it. Prevent it.

Rob: Me?

> *Rose:* You, Rob. You must tell him to call it off. You know Dave; he thinks he's doing it for you.
>
> But Rob turned again to the window and started again to trace his curlicues.
>
> 'No, Rose. I've had enough. Let happen happen. Let it all happen.'

Sources and contexts

Before I discuss the actors, I should say that I have the permission of those I interviewed to use the data collected in research studies as I see fit; in the context, that is, of my commitment to maintain the confidences and anonymities of those lives fictionalized here. I spent many hours with Rob and Rose, but we talked of things that do not appear here. Rob, Rose and others you meet in *Rob* do not – and should not – recognize themselves (unless I have done a poor job of storying my imaginings of their lives).

'Rob' and 'Rose' I met in the early 1990s as part of my work as a university tutor when I interviewed them both for many hours (though we never discussed the events that conspire to make this story). I worked with Rob and Rose specifically on the school's initiative to do something about the substantial number of kids who were losing their way in school. I came to know them very well, to be able to joke with Rose about her 'worthiness' and Rob about his 'kid-cred'. They were stars, the pair of them, and I interviewed them formally a number of times because I had a notion to write a paper about the power of their stewardship of the school, based – as I saw it then – on a shared commitment to schooling which I thought was essentially Fabian. I was aware, too, of the vulnerabilities which threatened them; I came – I think – to know well the shape of their thoughts, the edges of their fears. Rose, I should say, loved Rob, though I can't for a moment imagine that she ever made this known to him. He would never have had any idea of this. Rob loved his job, and certainly never Michelle.

'Dave Bird' I met in the late 1970s before ever I knew Rob and Rose, a lean man hungry actually not so much for celebrity as simple identity; a man licensed by a station – far above his ideas – to prosecute a justification for his own weaknesses. I was actually assaulted in the school in which I worked as a class teacher by a 14-year-old girl, and my union – through 'Dave' – showed an obscene excitement for the 'case' (which allied me ultimately with my assailant). Some may not recognize such a character as a 'typical' union representative, but when I needed to write about how Rob's teacher union had dealt with *his* 'case', it was Dave Bird who sprang immediately to mind, and so I imported him into this story. Bird is an amalgam of my personal experience, memory and imagination.

The 'interview' with the parents of 'Mark Whatisname' is data-driven, too. I have many tape-recorded interviews with the parents of children from a school for emotional and behavioural difficulties (EBD, a technical 'category' in the UK following the Education Act 1981) and the event in the story of *Rob* is drafted from a particular case where, time and again, the wretched and frightened mother kept saying: 'We don't want no trouble, Mr Clough; we've had enough trouble'. Mark is a 'walk-on' character in this story – and, indeed, is 'Whatsisname' – because I sensed that in the 'real' story of *Rob* he was a cypher, no more. As I choose to tell it, this is largely true for 'Michelle' in this story, too. 'Michelle' I never met – except that I have met many Michelles in different schools, at different parties.

Michelle and Mark are effectively absent – ironically, for they mark the beginning of the story – and Bird too is 'a minor'. They are all three crudely caricatured – because as characters they are marginal for me. It is only their actions that are important.

I have tried to schematize (in Table 8.1) something of the data-sources of this story. It is a makeshift device in which I posit 'units of meaning' – understood for my purposes as various aspects of narrative structure – and refer these to their origins in (variously) empirical contexts. I have not attempted to define, critically locate or otherwise problematize any of my terms, and so their uses may be questionable in this context. The list here is incomplete, but indicative.

As to the events which structure the story, the spitting incident is a fair account which I think a police officer might have given. I witnessed something similar when I visited a school in the late 1980s. Just so, *in outline* what I persuade *happened* to Rob is sustainable in the largely oblique LEA record. Just over a year after I had finished my work with Rob and Rose, I heard an account of what had 'happened' from a colleague.

The drama takes place mostly on Rose's and Rob's stage. What matters in this story – I think – is the failure of belief between two people. While Rose and Rob could believe in each other, the school survived, if not thrived. But there's a point – marked, I think, by Rose's thrilled statement about 'The glimpse of violence . . . that unwitting glance' which records something about an index of moral horror far more telling than any formal audit. A collapse of faith, perhaps.

What I find in the story

If the press is to be believed, schools in the UK (and possibly everywhere else in the world) are in states of crisis; it seems that almost every day somewhere in the press is reported a crisis of one form or another – of schooling generally, but specifically of finance, of teacher recruitment and education; of

Table 8.1 Schematization of the data-sources of 'Rob'

'Unit of meaning'	*Data source*	*Data/method*
Character/ 'Rob Joynson'	A, Deputy headteacher; interviewed (by PC; total of 11 hours) Sept.–Dec. 1992	Transcribed interview
Character/ 'Rose Thorpe'	B, Headteacher; interviewed (by PC; total of 7 hours) Sept.–Nov. 1992	Transcribed interview
Character/ 'Dave Bird'	C, Regional union representative; met (by PC) May 1979	Personal experience/ memory/imagination
Character/ 'Jan Hirst'	D, wife of 'Rob Joynson'; met (by PC) at dinner Dec. 1992	Memory/projection
Character/ Mark's parents	E and F, parents of child interviewed (by PC) for prospective place at residential special school (EBD), 1977	Memory/school files
Event/ spitting	Witnessed (by PC) on teaching practice supervision, Feb. 1988	Memory/student files
Event/ union actions	Events in XY School, 1993–94	School/local education authority (LEA)/union records; local press accounts

under/achievement by race and/or gender; of literacy and numeracy; of 'standards' in 'failing' schools; particularly and increasingly, of discipline and of violence – to name but some. Some albeit superficial indication of this state may be seen in a search which I carried out through the electronic archive of the *Times Educational Supplement* (TES), the UK's weekly title devoted exclusively to matters educational. The search of copy from 1994 to 1998 revealed 101 articles with the word *crisis* in their title; narrowing the focus for my purposes, the search further cited 31 articles entitled with the word *violence*, and 27 with the words *attack* or *assault* (though it must be acknowledged that some of these latter referred to strategic policy responses to phenomena such as teacher under-recruitment)!

The 'crisis of behaviour' is compelling: news accounts proliferate of student (and parental) attacks on teachers, somewhat less of teacher attacks on children but surely of a general and widespread breakdown of 'discipline' (variably correlated with, and illustrated by, factors such as substance abuse, bullying, race and gender, and teacher stress); analytic interpretations, aetiologies and rhetorical registers of panic vary according to ideologies, of course (see Haydon 1997 for an excellent account of the political construction of educational crises).

A number of reported cases of violent student behaviour has excited the UK media since the late 1990s, and we have seen national news bulletins occupied sometimes for several days with a particular 'case' as one of their lead stories. Cover of these cases draws in teachers, parents, school governors, local government officers, prominent educationists – and always, conspicuously, the teacher unions, whose role in the exposure of such phenomena is often creative. The scenes in Rob's kitchen and Rose's office are those that I imagine take place on the inside of these newspaper versions of crises of violence in schools.

The crisis of behaviour is compelling; it excites stereotypical responses from lay and professional, from left and right. But when the shouting is done – the crisis overcome or contained – the phenomena remain but their human provenance stays relatively unexplored or reported. Reasons for this lie not merely with the inexorable moving on of the news machine, but surely also with the confidential nature of many such cases, and the experience of crisis is seldom revealed.

It is hard to 'do justice' to the experience of these crises, for they are certainly just that in the lives of the actors through whom institutional fractures are played out. Any number of forms of representation could capture something of – say – the disintegration of a 'failing' school, or the historically accessible events which made up the ('true') story of *Rob*; but *evoking* the experience of crisis, rather than *explaining* it (see Trinh 1991: 162) calls for a richly persuasive rather than didactic account. The present story aspires to that task and tone.

A reading of Bev

Listen to this. It's a sort of poem:

There is shit everywhere. Because he has tried to reach the bathroom there is shit in a trail across the carpet and – though she does not find this for several days – there is shit on a pile of folded curtains by the top of the stairs.

* * *

I don't know what the real conclusion to this story is, for it's not a story simply exhausted by Bev's death. But with the passage of time the story has assembled itself from a clutch of data and – nude of any critical clothes – is simple enough. What is left when the data – the given – are returned to their owners is something simple and terrible; something grave and constant in human suffering. And schooling, it seems to me, is all but theorized by Bev's body.

Sources and contexts

As the previous readings have shown, the central character in each of *Klaus*, *Molly* and *Rob* is drawn substantially from one single individual's life story. *Bev* represents a departure from this loose mimesis; its sources are two separate characters whose lives are collapsed into one for the moral and political purposes of my story.

In Chapter 1 I wrote about my attempts to 'reproduce' Nick, a teacher with whom I worked on the Economic and Social Research Council-funded project *Constructions of Special Educational Need* (a fuller account is to be found in Clough 1995). As a narrative line, it is still Nick's story which provides the frame for *Bev*, but the central character is changed (not least in gender) and filled out with aspects of another life. This other life – the original 'Bev' – is drawn from a woman I worked with in the mid-1970s, who did indeed die from self-neglect. (I fear that my story makes something of a bosomy, mother-earth remedial teacher caricature of her; but, then, I think that's what she proudly aspired to be – and what was her great virtue – in the cultural context of 1970s special schooling.)

In Clough (1995), Nick's is an unfinished story, a fragment used to illuminate, among other things, something of the event of transgressive data; *Bev* both completes and updates the story. *Bev* is elaborated from the same school contexts as *Molly* and in some ways represents another 'take' on the situation which is described there. But it is only recently, however, that the story has assembled itself with the particular shape and purpose which it now has.

The present form of the story came, in fact, as my response to policy contexts and events some 10 years removed from experiences in that school. In the late 1990s there began to emerge in the media stories of how the offical inspection of schools was undermining not only teacher morale but also the actual health of staff.

In June 1997 the then new Secretary of State for Education, David Blunkett, identified 18 schools said to be failing their pupils. In November of the same year the Secretary of State was reported to be prepared to do the same again. David Blunkett said:

> I make no apology for it and we will continue doing it whatever anyone says.
>
> (Gardiner 1997)

The TES reported that Blunkett denied that the 'naming and shaming' process was intended to humiliate or that teachers should be treated differently from other 'service industries':

> We would never use the term 'humiliation' in transport or industry. We would not wonder if it upset a train driver if you asked if he was competent to drive.
>
> (Gardiner 1997)

Headteachers and teacher unions came out vociferously against 'shaming' and eventually it was announced that 'shaming' was to be abandoned as a policy to encourage improvement. The Secretary of State was reported as saying:

> teachers were doing a first-rate job [and] in future would be doing it with Government support.
>
> (Rafferty et al. 1998)

But there are stories beneath the headlines; stories of the lives of teachers, headteachers, and doubtless of parents and pupils. The headteacher of one such school was reported in the TES as saying that being named had hindered rather than accelerated the school's progress, describing the government's action as 'a devastating kick in the teeth' (Gardiner 1997). The questions that life-historical research can ask and – in part answer – is: What lies behind these headlines? What is it like to be the headteacher of a school 'named and shamed' as failing to do its duty for its pupils?

Something of the character and the effects of another government policy for improvement is to be seen in the reporting of the impact of an Office for Standards in Education (Ofsted) inspection upon headteachers, their lives and their schools. Examples of cases reported in the TES included that of a *former* headteacher whose school was placed in 'special measures' by Ofsted in November 1997. The report tells of the consequent end of the headteacher's 12-year headship (as a result of parental pressure following the damning Ofsted report). The headteacher is reported to have felt the pressure of the parents' campaign against her and her feeling of powerlessness in the face of it:

> when the snowball starts to roll no one can stop it. People turn against you for no apparent reason.
>
> In the end, there were so many nasty letters coming to me I didn't think the school was safe. So for the sake of the school I resigned.
>
> It's not so much that I feel bitter personally, but it's a massive injustice that's going on in our society. As a school we did a lot more than was ever said and we were achieving more than we were ever given credit for. The children were working so hard and did not deserve to be told they were failing.
>
> (Pyke 1998)

Another headteacher was reported to have suffered a breakdown due to his experience of Ofsted inspection at his school. The TES reported it thus:

> Mr Harries' life now lies in tatters. He has contemplated suicide; he has received psychiatric counselling; he is still taking antidepressants for the nervous breakdown . . .

Mr Harries, 47, a father of two, is unable to work again. His doctor diagnosed reactive depression and post-traumatic stress disorder. He was forced to take early retirement due to ill health from his job as headteacher.

(Mendick 1998)

Such reports provide the 'hint' of what might be happening in the life of this man and his family, indeed of his school. This man is quoted as saying:

The thing you felt so proud of is suddenly a source of shame and there is nothing worse than that. For a long time I couldn't cope at all. I couldn't even mow the lawn.

(Mendick 1998)

If the media reports of teacher stress tell us anything, they certainly indicate that there is *something* to be asked about the present circumstances in which many teachers work. In 2000 it was reported that inspection stress had been linked to the death of at least four teachers in the previous two years. The cases highlighted included the suicide of a 57-year-old teacher after a critical report from Ofsted, and a 29-year-old teacher who hanged himself *prior* to an Ofsted inspection (Mansell 2000). 'Teacherline', a telephone helpline for teachers experiencing stress, received over 6000 calls in the first six months of operation, with one in four of the workplace issues teachers raised being related to stress, anxiety or depression (Passmore 2000).

Clearly there is much more to the stories behind the lives which are briefly depicted in newspaper reports, and this attests to the importance of life-story work which can tell the real stories of teachers' lives and experiences, and the relationship of their work to the 'rest' of their lives and relationships.

What do I find in the story?

Bev is an attempt to crystallize and symbolize some of the issues around institutional and personal disintegration, though it was only much later that I gave them the topical significance that they now have. (And this seems to me to be a good example of the benefits of sometimes leaving data to mature.) But although these significances were yet to be created, I was nevertheless taken at the time by the inchoate saliences of the research setting.

So, beyond these substantive issues, I think that as a research text the story challenges the very nature and means of production of data; for, as St Pierre (1997: 176) has it, 'if data are the foundation on which knowledge rests, it is important to trouble the common-sense understanding of that signifier in post-foundational research that aims to produce different knowledge and to produce knowledge differently' (see also Lather and Smithies 1997; Meiners 1999). Thus the proto-story (of Nick) came from non-mediate data, and I recorded something of this 'transgressive' process of creation:

After three days of looking for Nick [in the transcriptions] I found him in my imagination . . . But what I wrote was made in my own store of 'knowledge' and, free of the 'facts', seemed to say more of Nick and Nick in school than ever he had said or could have said. [For] in excitedly attaching the organism/organization idea, and eagerly attaching badges to analyse that relationship, I had forgotten my own insertion in this particular culture: the organism that was/is me and which would inevitably mediate whatever I saw and felt. And my 'understanding of others' – in this case Nick and his school – came not from the data spilling from the tea-chests, nor from any reading of the literature but, indeed, from a setting aside of those things; and from a simple act of imagination that could only have sprung from my own experience. It doesn't matter whether what I wrote about Nick took place in fact; it takes place in an act of imagination driven by profound symbols; the event symbolises in a way which data and analysis could never do.

(Clough 1995: 134)

And in a similar way, the curious passage which opens the story provides another example of 'transgressive' data disposed to research ends.

A reading of Lolly

You pull on a thread and little suspect how the whole weave puckers.
  In 1992 I plucked a thread from the weave of lives I was then interested in. On Tuesday 22 February 2001, the chickens came home, not in search of a quiet perch but wild-eyed, the-worm-turned, and full of wrath.

* * *

Lol was still stood against the window, silent, looking out on the silent street. He raised an indifferent finger to the window and drew a line indifferently across the scars of earlier sketches on the condensation. When he turned, I was little with fear in my chair.

  'What do you want? What can I do? Say, Lol – what d'you want?'

In the back room I heard the phone ring three times and then Phil's voice a room away, faintly.

  'Lol, please.'

Lol stayed with his back to the window, quite motionless.

  'Lol, what do you want?'

And then he moved slowly across the room till he stood above me, looking down.

'Nothing,' he said finally. 'Nothing.'

The door opened and as Phil made to come in, I tried to stand. Phil made to speak, but was arrested by what he saw, mouth quite open: Lol towering above me, me trying to stand, a patch of wet across my groin and down to one knee.

'Nothing. Or perhaps . . .'

and he spread his hands to take in me, Phil, the room and all:

'Or perhaps this.'

And was gone. I am done with stories.

Sources and contexts

Lolly is a dismal and ironic triumph; roosters come home indeed, worms turned, as a sort of rough justice asserts the subtle materialism of ethics.

This (fifth) story emerged in quite a different way from the others and, unlike them, is a complete fiction. The first four emerged as fairly self-conscious narrativizations (Mink 1978) of events and hunches which, as I have alerted, seemed to serve some quite particular – and obvious – moral and political purposes (identical, of course, with methodological intent). This fifth, on the other hand, has its origins in dialogues prompted by the earlier stories. It is in large part a response – in suitably narrative form – to some of the criticisms which have been made of my stories.

Taken together, the first four stories have much in common. They deal commonly in wretchedness. (I have often been asked why I write stories of 'terror' and 'darkness' – why I don't write positive and uplifting stories as well – create a balance. But understanding 'difficulty' is my work, I work with/in the field of educational, social and moral difficulty – thus the stories themselves are difficult.) As I choose to tell these tales, their common narrator is a researcher with an interest in 'difficult' lives, careers and institutions, and the stories mostly reflect his experiences of encountering and trying to make sense of the lives he records for a living. From the outset, in the story of *Klaus*, it is clear that 'making sense' means fitting these lives into the researcher's own personal world of experiences and values; and as the stories (separately) unfold he is always found in some sort of struggle to understand the relation of personal and professional. Of course there is a tangle between this 'character' of the researcher who narrates the stories and myself. But I choose to use this character, too, to explore the depth of difficulty as well as the parameters of method.

The first, *Klaus*, features his encounter as a young teacher with a child with emotional and behavioural difficulties, and with his father. The second, *Molly*, is based on the ethnographic study of a bunch of 'bad lads', while the third, *Rob*, records the inevitable fate of a teacher who makes a stand against increasing disorder. In the fourth, *Bev*, a teacher and her school appear to disintegrate together. Though none of the stories happened precisely as told, they are all made from events which are real enough; made with the data of interview, life-historical reflection, observational and other inquiry; enriched with transgressive data from my own experience; and 'knit with symbolic equivalents' (Yalom 1991: ix) which maintain the reality, while concealing the identity, of actual people (see also McLeod 1997).

As each of the first four stories emerged, I took opportunities to share them with various seminar and conference audiences. Frequently responses to the stories included questions like:

Are these 'real' people? If so . . . then what right have you to characterize them in this way, or that?

Or:

Do they know you've written about them like this?

And:

So . . . where were you in all this? 'Hanging out'? . . . a mere 'recording intelligence'?

For all that they were mostly gently put, these questions were often freighted with grievance (which was not always an unequivocal proxy).

The fifth story emerged from these sessions and their questions, and specifically from a seminar with a particular group of Masters' students who were roused by the story of *Molly*. How dared I . . .? How could I . . .? Who was I to . . .? And one student in particular was little short of tears as *Molly* forced reconnection to the experience of his 14-year-old son and the raw possibility that I could have been 'using' him as data.

So a fifth story was written, partly to respond to and partly to explore some of these very embodied, angry ethical concerns; and to do so in the medium of the original stories (that is, without recourse to a critical text, or meta-story). But thematically, the story also has a distinct artistic purpose: it completes the suite for, while integral as a fiction in its own right, *Lolly: the final word* also 'plays back' on the concerns and characters of the earlier stories.

What do I find in the story?

> People tend to forget that my presence runs counter to their best inter-
> est . . . Writers are always selling somebody out.
>
> (Didion 1968: xiv)

One of the things which the story does is to throw into urgent relief the
whole business of whether – and how – these are true stories. If they are – if,
that is, these are real people involved in real events – then those real people
are betrayed by these accounts; as Lolly says, 'that was *my* mother . . . *my*
mother'. And if they are not? Then they are mere fictions, more or less effective as fictions are. Of course *Lolly* did not happen. But what is subtly terri-
fying about it is – to the extent that it 'works' – that it *could* have happened.
Plausibility, to the extent that it connects with our fear of 'chickens coming
home to roost', is a key element here. There is no protection in this story –
no silver lining – just raw confrontation.

The story also revisits and reviews some of the issues of power relations
raised through all the stories, though particularly in *Molly*. And it is significant that it is Lolly who has 'the final word' (and, indeed, the narrator is
'done with stories').

All of this comes back to what is being attempted here, and what claims
are being made about the truth of those attempts (Barone 1998). I shall look
more systematically at such claims to truth in the final two chapters (9 and
10) where I return to contemporary debate about social and educational
research, and offer a position on the location of narrative within that debate.
Chapter 10 takes the form of an essay in which I stand back from direct
presentation and discussion of the stories, and argue more conventionally
for the place of fictional writing in educational and social research.

Note

1 'It could be said of me that in this book I have only made up a bunch of other
men's flowers, providing of my own only the string that ties them together' (Montaigne (1580) *Essais*, Book 3, Chapter 12, ed. M. Rat, 1958).

9 | Narratives of educational practice

> One goal [of educational research] must be to produce accounts which
> deny the reader [the] comfort of a shared ground with the author, fore-
> ground ambivalence and undermine the authority of their own assertions.
> (Stronach and MacLure 1998: 57)

In this chapter I relate the meaning and value of stories in educational settings to some current disquiets about educational research generally. My
argument is essentially one about the nature and role of language in the
creation of research processes and findings.

The criticisms of educational research forefronted by Tooley (1998)
among others are well noticed in the current literature. Their common
observations are familiar enough: educational research is parochial, frag-
mented and lacking rigour; it is fitful in its occupations and fails to accumu-
late; the means of production reflect huge discontinuities between researcher
and researched (and hence theory and practice) – and so on. The arguments
are familiar enough, indeed, to point up that their net effect is not a radical
and critical discovery so much as a tired rehearsal of truisms (and Pring
2000 deals particularly fittingly with these). What I should like to add to
these debates is something of a corrective whose truth is probably taken for
granted in our common understandings of how research is made by people;
this corrective is a reassertion of the vitally constitutive role of language.
(Actually, a reading of Carr and Kemmis (1986) discovers many of these
concerns adumbrated without the dubious decoration of postmodernism.)

There are, for argument's sake, two contrary directions in educational
research at this time, and they suggest movements in polarized directions.
The one, for argument's sake, largely takes its terms and instruments for
granted, and all that remains is to gather data to feed those designs which
are given with the instruments – for example in many large-scale funded
programmes; this is a process, then, of *addition*, and it is an endless process.
The other – for this argument's sake – is that more recent occupation of
educational research with the researcher themself, and their very insertion
in the process of research; this activity endlessly problematizes terms and

instruments, and so is a process of *subtraction*; of taking away, that is, the methodologically impure, the ideologically suspect.

This antinomy of outward and inward direction seems to me to be of much more use – because of its greater moral importance – than many of the traditional and merely contingent ones (such as qualitative/quantitative, subjective/objective and so on) though they may be logically cognate. But cognition is a trick here; it matters more that these traditional polarizations are not morally necessitated. They are functions of method which does not, of itself, carry any moral charge; and it is surely the drive to some revelation of the author's moral engagement with their topic that lies (or should lie) behind this baggage-stripping trend of self-conscious research.

In Chapter 8 (in 'A reading of Klaus') I drew attention to examples of research which emphasized the reflective self in educational inquiry (Burgess 1985; Walford 1991; Clough and Barton 1995; Clough 1998; Clough and Corbett 2000) and to the location and justification of such disclosure in a particular tradition of human science study. In respect of the latter, Walford's reminder that most such self-conscious inquiry is undertaken by qualitatively oriented researchers raises the question whether quantitative procedures may not be susceptible to this sort of treatment. But if this is so – which I doubt anyway – then it is not because such researchers are not brought morally to their work, but that those forms of inquiry appear to depend for their validity on a supremacy of method policed with a total suppression of personal engagement.

Of course, an undoubted effect of the Research Assessment Exercise (RAE) is that many research studies have lost clear connectedness with epistemology and ontology; this is to say that they proceed along safe, well-sedimented channels which take their objects and the instruments which investigate them for granted; there may be curiosity but seldom if ever any radical astonishment, or concern really to problematize phenomena in terms of their moral and political colour. 'Safety' (as in accepted method), I suggest, may often stand in the way of research and the moral/political act. Of course, examples to the contrary may be drawn in to contradict my argument, but essentially 'outcomes' remain in favour over 'problematization' (see Hamilton 1998).

Contextualization of the study in hand tends to be confined to a limited and endlessly inter- and intra-referring literature which shores up its own claims. And it is customary to show how 'clean' were the instruments used by arguing their distinctness from us as persons; look, we would typically say, they have been used as techniques by researchers before us; and as they are not of them so they are not of us. So all the drive of this 'methodology' is towards saying: look, there is no infection here. But this emphasis on instrumentation means the danger also that what is ultimately missing from the study is any real engagement of values – for instruments do not themselves have values. As ethnography discovers its eighth, ninth, tenth (?)

moments (Lincoln 1995; Denzin and Lincoln 2000), perhaps, so too will 'messiness' of method emerge as a 'respectable' form of understanding. But while measures, statistics and sterility of research instruments exist, research which tells stories of the moral and political in educational settings will remain peripheral.

It is not incidental that the research report is, in the main, a text characterized by an austerity of language which makes it hard to read; it is traditionally in the nature of research to suppress the so-called subjective responses of the researcher, or at least to force these within the frame of a morally indifferent scheme. The researcher puts instruments between themself and their objects. They have to, because the researcher must show that their understanding always refers to a scheme of things constituted by the community. It can hardly be surprising, then, that in the research report the communicative functions of language are elevated over its expressive qualities. The language of research must serve to render the object not as the researcher sees it in experience, but as a research community would have it, as re-presented by so many data whose validity can be checked and referenced. These checks, these references, maintain the language of the tribe, and thus control the development of its vocabulary.

Some case studies, some ethnographies give the lie to this view. But if you look at how they do this – how the ones which really 'work' for you do this – then surely it is because they strain at their own given form; they seek to push back the restraints of given form, to form anew, to innovate form on pain of failing to express what the writer feels must be expressed. And where these studies work, there is surely some surplus of meaning over the cold lexical qualities which language usually demonstrates in the research report.

For what is it, ultimately, that is persuasive about this or that piece of research? It is surely not – at the level of experience – its claim to 'validity'. We are not led in the first instance to affirm a piece of research because of any elegance of validation, but by its manifest (and manifestly taken-for-granted) ability to speak to our experience because it shares our objects. For what is research in educational settings *for* if it is not to *understand*; and when we understand, we can change (Bolton 1981).

These 'objects' are of course constructed differently by different people, and although the nature of the object will *of itself* indicate a particular mode of inquiry, the role of individual consciousness in actually constituting that object for specific moral and political purposes is radical. As Pring (2000) says,

> The object of research will necessarily be seen differently by different practitioners (and by different traditions of practice within which they work) as they select different cultural resources for inspiration and different forms of life to aspire to.
>
> (Pring 2000: 158)

For we are a long way from realizing that research in the social sciences will find in its theatres of inquiry only what it puts there. (And this is particularly true in my own field of educational difficulty, whose origins in the measurement of behaviour endure as stark functions of policy.) For 'educational practices' are pre-eminently worlds of paid-up meanings – as it were – and attributions; in experience they issue from and are set about with meanings which are always ready-to-hand. And as researchers of educational practices, we ourselves give shape, weight and identity to these meanings: we do not come innocent to a task or situation of events; rather, we wilfully situate those events not merely in the institutional meanings which our profession provides but also, and in the same moment, we constitute them as expressions of ourselves. Inevitably, the energies of our own psychic and social history fuel our insight, and leave traces of those earlier meanings. But because the institutional drive requires a publicly accountable knowledge, we resort to method to clarify – though in fact mostly obscure – our true involvement.

Stronach and MacLure (1998) suggest that even this methodological aspiration is deeply frustrated, and indeed that

> it is in those accounts which seem most 'natural', 'transparent', 'real' or 'rounded' that are most carefully wrought with a view to producing just those effects in the reader – that the writer is never more present in the text than when she seems to be absent, and the subject seldom less audible than when he seems to be speaking for himself . . . The appearance of artlessness is a rather artful business.
>
> (Stronach and MacLure 1998: 35)

For we might suppose that we slip method between us and those events, a sort of prophylactic which will keep them distinct from us. But this is to misunderstand the nature of method and its seamless identity with what it only apparently treats of. Science begins, says Oakeshott (1933: 37), 'only when the world of things opened to us by our sense and perceptions has been forgotten or set on one side.' The scientific way of seeing is identical with what it sees in its search for stability:

> The method and the matter of scientific knowledge are not two parties . . . they are inseparable aspects of a single whole . . . And the notion of the categories of scientific knowledge or the instruments of scientific measurement interposing themselves between the scientist and his object is a notion utterly foreign to the character of scientific experience. Without the categories and the method, there is no matter; without the instruments of measurement, nothing to measure. *'Nature' is the product not the datum of scientific thought.*
>
> (Oakeshott 1933: 37, added emphasis)

The datum becomes, then, not the consequence of a way of seeing even, but that act itself (and as such, must be intentionally opposed to the thing in itself). And in just this way are 'educational practices' produced by research. For there are no instruments, no methods prior to the function of consciousness, and all instruments and measures depend for their very existence on the way they serve this function. Consciousness seeks objects – indeed is knowable only by the moment and way of its finding them. And the whole of this experience is organized through an aesthetic.

Aesthetic attending to something is not a special or a marginal case peculiar to (self-conscious) artists, but one which can be systematically developed – and indeed marketed – by them only because it is the very foundation of intelligence. This is to say no more than that we attend primarily to objects in this way as a condition of our being in the world; we are here and embodied. But in the research experience we find ourselves occupied by a concern with the more patent and accountable forms of truth given with intellectual or material schemes. The 'research attitude', predicated on scientific principles, is methodologically opposed to art in its concern with explicitation and justification. For, as Bridges (1998) suggests:

> I am less concerned that educational research will contribute to social science (though this is a perfectly honourable aspiration) than that the thinking (the theory, if you like) which informs educational research is drawn from the richest and most radical seams of current and historical intellectual life. In my observation the theory that comes out of empirical research in education rarely represents much of an advance on the theory that went into it – or, to personalise the point, it is the intellectually most richly endowed researchers who seem to be able to provide the most stimulating and provocative analyses however modest the empirical research they engage in.
>
> (Bridges 1998: 85)

How do these arguments relate specifically to our uses of narrative in educational practices – and specifically those which seek to capture and politically deploy the lives of teachers and schools? Denzin (1989: 14) brings us back to the crucial role of language in these processes, for 'there is no clear window into the inner life of a person, for any window is always filtered through the glaze of language, signs and the process of signification' (see also Coates 1986; Swann 1992). The researcher's struggle, then, is not primarily with method; it is a struggle for language which will 'reawaken ethical and aesthetic sensitivities that, increasingly have been purged from the scientific discourse of too many educators' (Apple 1996: xiii). In this way, social research might be seen to be no more – and certainly no less – than a perpetual refinement of language (which is one way in which it is radically different from medical research: Hargreaves 1997). For, as Hamilton has it:

all humans still retain their investigative powers. They – or we – try to think ahead and, in all kinds of ways, probe the future. The pursuit of such domestication may seem remote from the mysteries of modern science.

(Hamilton 1998: 81)

The essential point is that educational researchers should assemble, within their research craft, an honesty and integrity of language with which to express the moral positions (as well as the methodological justifications) of their inquiry. This must inevitably call for new ways of seeing.

I give the final word in this chapter to Stronach and MacLure (1998):

There are good reasons, therefore, for attending to the forms in which teachers are portrayed in research accounts, whether by themselves or by other people. Narratives that promote coherence, singularity and closure, and which aim to set up a cosy camaraderie with the reader, are ultimately conservative and uncritical of prevailing ideological and representational arrangements. If we refuse to 'interrogate' these forms, we run the risk of promoting an uncritical research practice which, in seeming to describe teachers as they 'really are', simply perpetuates whatever iconographies of teacher-hood happen to be circulating in the various professional cultures (research practitioner, academic) at any given time.

(Stronach and MacLure 1998: 56–7)

10 | 'To the things themselves!'

I am concerned in this final chapter with how fictional writing may be seen as wholly legitimate educational and social science inquiry. I wish also to point up how persistent challenge to the received conceptual furniture of educational research is given with the very nature and process of the research act itself *if it truly addresses the objects of an 'educational practice'*. The scheme of the chapter depends first on a phenomenology of language (derived in the main from Merleau-Ponty 1962); second, on Hofstadter's (1965) account of forms of truth; and hence on a view of the contiguity *in experience* of the literary and ethnographic project. A major aim of the chapter is to argue for a view of fictional writing not as 'alternative' (or even particularly new), but rather as issuing from the same *radical* concerns and processes as those of other social scientists. As Postman puts this,

> Both a social scientist and a novelist give unique interpretations to a set of human events and support their interpretations with examples in various forms. Their interpretations cannot be proved or disproved, but will draw their appeal from the power of their language, the depth of their explanations, the relevance of their examples, and the credibility of their themes. And all this has, in both cases, an identifiable moral purpose.
>
> (Postman 1992: 154)

Of course, we shall not in the end arrive at an account of truth-in-fiction which will meet the orthodox criteria of a social science. Such an account would be absurd, much as we might as rigorously argue the existence of God. (Interestingly, in both cases, surely the question of existence is already answered, and the question is rather *how* this exists than *whether*.) It remains, however, in the examined world in which we live – where evidence genuinely matters – to offer some justification for the uses of fiction in social science which will help students to scoop with a scholarly confidence – 'without self-importance or self-consciousness' (Inglis 1969: 15) – deep into their personal resources for persuasive writing which cannot be dismissed as 'mere fiction'. To do this calls for a methodology which can deal analytic justice at the same time as experiential truth. This is a tall order.

But: when I turn on the radio or television, pick up a newspaper, a journal article or a novel, listen to a seminar presentation or watch a theatre play – in each case I attune myself quite precisely, yet with minimal effort or art, to a form of truth. That is to say, I am located in a version of truth whose engines are so far hidden from view that they are silent. It is, of course, only when I sense there is some fault that I begin to hear the noise of those engines, and reach perhaps for a set of tools which will detect, analyse – correct, even – the fault. For strings of words do not mean something because they are stuffed or laid out with propositional knowledge. They mean because those words glance off much more regressed knowledges – vapid certainties – which are only in later moments made angular with the furniture of analysis (the pixels of experience as it were suddenly organized with actual purpose from a dense galaxy of possible meanings).

What follows is an analysis of language which goes a part of the way to saying how stories – indifferently among any or all other forms of text – have meaning for us.

The experience of meaning

The experience of meaning and its historical senses are not continuous. It is mainly the latter with which social inquiry has occupied itself; phenomenology, on the other hand, is concerned to illuminate the experience, and in so doing disputes the creation of the very things (objects) which science takes for granted. But if the reality of things cannot be simply assumed, then what measures or instruments can be used to get to 'the things themselves'?

Consciousness is, of course, the starting-point; but then, consciousness is nothing without objects, since self and objects are constituted in the same moment. Those moments of constitution are finally the ground of phenomenology, then, and the phenomenological method could be described as a systematic attempt to recapitulate the events of meaning. This means that a phenomenology can be defined by its revelation not only of particular objects – 'a man' or 'honesty' or 'speaking', say – but also of how those objects are so constituted. By definition, such a description of objects would reveal the engagement of its author. This characterization needs expansion.

Consciousness provides objects

The science of phenomenology – for example, that of Merleau-Ponty (1962) – is greatly complicated by its self-consciousness; the general project to describe the history of experience is achieved only by working through the functions of consciousness, so we must think in order to write a phenomenology of thought, use language to talk about speech, and so on. This could be described as the first inhibition of phenomenology as a science. The second is the difficulty it has in justifying the claim to speak of a commonality of experience. Because no quantifying schemes can be applied to the transcendental terms it has in place of independent instruments, measures such as validity and reliability, for example, are not appropriate.

A phenomenology succeeds, however, by being a virtue before these detractions. There are no instruments, no measures prior to the very function of consciousness, and all instruments and all measures depend for their very existence on the way they serve this function. This is not to see consciousness as in any way prior to objects, or – as is often assumed – phenomenology as an essentially subjective project. On the contrary, consciousness *seeks* objects, indeed is known only by the moment and way of its finding them. So if consciousness or a phenomenology points out its objects to us, it is our recognition of those objects which recommends it, not the instruments of their discovery. As I noted in Chapter 9, we are not in the first instance led to affirm a view by some elaborate process of 'validation' but by its capacity to speak to our experience because it shares our objects. The 'controls' of a phenomenology are only those of consciousness, and are no more sophisticated; 'checks' are similarly constituted; does a particular account, Bolton asks (echoing Hume),

> contain any metaphor which reveals a reality deeper than common sense? No. Does it excite you to a moral involvement in the affairs with which it deals? No. Commit it then to the flames, for it is nothing but information that will soon be superceded by more information.
> (Bolton 1981: 9)

This is not to make a Luddite assault on instruments, but to remember that they are the products (and not the objects) of consciousness, and that consciousness first provided the circumstance of their ability to characterize reality. The 'crisis' of science which Husserl (1970) speaks of occurs when the foundational acts which abstract the object from pre-scientific experience are occluded, and nature is identified with its already constituted and quantifiable objects. Again, this is not a peevish criticism of science which would do away with its products willy-nilly; the point is that scientific observations are born in particular events, and may not necessarily be transferable. In his discussion of Galilean mathematics, Husserl says

> Actually the process whereby material mathematics is put into formal-logical form . . . is perfectly legitimate, indeed necessary. . . . But all this can and must be a method which is understood and practiced in a fully conscious way. It can be this, however, only if care is taken to avoid

dangerous shifts of meaning by keeping in mind *the original bestowal of meaning* upon the method, through which it has the sense of achieving knowledge about the world.

(Husserl 1970: 47, added emphasis)

The particular and the general

It is the sense of a particular time which is missing from the social scientific account as much as the print of the originator; what is *scientifically* true holds indifferently across contexts of situation. But *events* are unique by definition, and however identical in their phenomenal setting, their participants or their aims, it remains that consciousness is indispensably variable in its presence at the event, and no two events can share that constitution. This is finally to say that events are defined as correlates of human intentions, and that their character is imperfectly revealed by any process of history-making. In particular, any way of characterizing an event should be suggested by the peculiarities of the event itself, and lose its justification as the event itself recedes in time. (This is, of course, a methodological truism commonly rehearsed in most critical justification of quantitative method.)

What, then, of those features of events which show themselves so consistently across contexts that we feel we can extrapolate them as constant or transcendent elements and hence meet them with standard methods? Again, the force of Husserl's comment is not that we cannot have such features, but that we should remember how the power of such terms was achieved, and understand the nature of their purchase on the world. After Kant, we can say that a way of seeing becomes transcendent when it appears to organize discourse around a given domain of experience. But such ways of seeing are cultural products which may come to enjoy a cultural life out of sight of their human origination, hallowed by use rather than vision. The possibility of a distinction between use and value here is arguable. The argument of relativist philosophers (such as Kuhn 1970) that we are educated into ways of seeing which condition our values is at least *practically* acceptable. It is similarly *effectively* true of science that it misunderstands the nature of its products. No scientists would want to claim that they deal with a naked reality, but this does not excuse science as a virtual community from operating *as if* what it worked on were real.

But as Oakeshott (1933: 37) reminds us, ' "Nature" is the product not the datum of scientific thought'. The datum becomes, then, not the consequence of a way of seeing even, but that act itself, and as such must be intentionally opposed to the thing in itself. In this opposition we discover the nature of the particular. For science attempts to conceive of the world 'under the category of quantity' (Oakeshott 1933: 37) and its datum has the required stability only by virtue of the categorical set of which it is an indifferent member. There can, by this definition, be no such scientific experience as that *of the particular*. Again, Whitehead (1948: 108) describes the aim of science to 'seek objects with the most permanent definite simplicity of character.'

Lived consciousness, on the other hand, dwells only in the particular, the general being what Oakeshott (1933: 43) calls an *arrest of experience*. The category of quantity is nowhere of the essence of the thing which, because it always patently exceeds the noetic acts which characterize it, remains to be experienced in its individual and materially distinct self. (Husserl (1960) distinguishes the *noesis* – the act of perception – from the *noema*, the percept as it is given to the subject. This is further distinct from *the object itself*.)

The category of quantity can be said to reveal a kind of essence, but only of the kind which is indifferently shared by members of a set which is defined by the discipline of the inquiry. But if the 'essential essence' – as Heidegger (1962: 194) calls it – is not characterized by a numerical account, it is equally true that words are not up to accomplishing its intuited aesthetic presence either. In any event, the relation between words and numbers is not one of mutual exclusion, and the opposition of the quantitative and the qualitative is expedient rather than real. If it is true that scientific instruments create matter, it is equally true of words that they reveal or accomplish something intentionally, but in cooperation with the real world. In emphasizing the expressive character of words we are tacitly denying any sense of an instrumental or technological function. Any priority claimed for words is on the strength of their aesthetic foundation as actual responses to the physical world. Their inability to 'fix' reality is the condition of their being in the fluid field of embodied consciousness. Numbers are no less intentional, but their objects are *noemata*, and they qualify the cultural products which words create rather than share the same world from which words arise; number do not have real referents. But the result of this distinction should not be to elevate words – and the qualitative – over numbers – and the quantitative – for most practice proceeds unselfconsciously without any such explicit methodological commitment. But it points to a way of validating inquiry which does not itself require validation. This is by asking whether and how an inquiry is *object directed*.

'To the things themselves!' (Husserl 1960)

Objects are defined as those real things which, by virtue of their independence of consciousness, require this consciousness to identify them. Acts and artefacts of identification *(noeses* and *noemata)* belong to consciousness as correlates of the object which, on pain of ceasing to exist, must perpetually exceed the descriptions which are themselves properties and consciousness. By this definition objects are unchanging, flux being a condition of consciousness and not of things. So an object-directed inquiry is not one which changes the object, but which somehow articulates the change of engage-ment of its author with their objects. Any report which 'changes' objects is a legerdemain which disguises the event of the inquirer's findings; all dis-covery, we could say (adapting Merleau-Ponty), is self-discovery, 'failing which it could have no objects' (Merleau-Ponty 1962: 191). So research is *not* object directed if, failing to declare the interests of consciousness, it assumes that its characterizations are real. For it *they* are, then the object is indifferently at the mercy of such characterizations to be whatever fashion or expediency require it to be. That being so, there is no longer any moral requirement of inquiry to describe the real as it is.

For morality itself is described by the manner in which consciousness entertains objects. This is not a special understanding of the word, but pre-cisely what is implied, if not made explicit, in all its uses. MacMurray (1935: 62) makes this point clearly: right and wrong have to do with seeing the object *as it is in itself*, and not *as I would have it 'for me'*. This is no less true in the affective than in the material sphere of experience, and MacMurray distinguishes love of the other *as he really is* from 'love' for him *as I need him to be*. In any event morality is concerned with taking responsibility for one's attitude to an object, be it a person or a situation or a thing, and with therefore separating its attributes from one's (intentional) own. This is not schizoid finally because the will has precisely the project of ever approxi-mating characterizations with their objects. Morality enables us to distin-guish in human terms between different manners of being-towards objects. When MacMurray (1935: 63) observes that 'Reason is primarily an affair of the emotions', he does not mean that morality is finally arbitrary, or 'merely personal'; rather chastity ('emotional honesty') derives from openness to the reality of objects sensibly held, and not merely intellectually abstracted, and sedimented.'

The problem of evaluation

We are led from this consideration to ask about an inquiry, not 'Is it quali-tative or quantitative?', but 'Is it moral?' There remains a problem of evalu-ation. For even if an inquiry is 'open to its objects', if it declares the values and unique method of its author how do we know that, and what yardstick can we possibly find which will qualitatively determine its morality? And anyway, if it deals in such a particular way with the particular, what can we compare it with and what relevance could it have for general experience? Is this not likely to be the very worst of 'subjectivity'?

By opposing subjectivity with objectivity we distinguish persons from objects in such a way that their relation cannot be described without recourse to extremes of mentalist or behaviourist philosophy. If, on the other hand, we understand the terms as continuously related ways of *having* objects, then we take the vital step of involving persons with objects by necessity. *Subjectivity is defined, then, not by the particular which it dwells in by virtue of its own uniqueness, but by the concern it shows to give that particular a general recognition.* Such recognition completes the act, and the particular becomes an object constituted by sharing.

This process is not susceptible to validation. Because it has not explained subject–object relations for its schemes, the 'research attitude' – to which validation as a technique belongs – naively assumes this relation and is to be found acting in the firm reality of *noemata*.

Of course, this research attitude is right when it speaks of demanding validation in terms of the object and not of the inquirer; it is right in supposing that the object is firm and, even if constituted, that it pre-exists characterization. But the real meaning of its 'objectivity' is revealed when, in its provision of the validation it required, it fails to distinguish between the object proper and the characterizations given by what are yet more *noemata*. Again, validation needs endless shoring up with ever-regressing devices because it is not object directed.

We have said that a phenomenology can be known by its revelation of the author's engagement with their objects. But how precisely do we know that? This is still the question. And what is it which we recognize and affirm or dispute?

If we return to the genesis of the phenomenology, we observe that there is a researcher and there is a *situation of objects* which they must constitute. Now at this point there occurs a critical *moment of characterization* which determines these objects for the researcher and for the researcher's audience. This is the moment normally referred to as methodological, and which as such is the correlate of the later process of validation. Indeed, it is all that validation can reveal: is the *method* what it set out to be, what its author says it is? For validation is based, as we shall see, on a limited model of truth which either takes for granted, or else ignores, the earlier process of *verification* which guarantees its coherence.

Validation depends on further regressed devices in quite the way that truth of statement and truth of things – conceptual and pragmatic truths – depend on things being already what/as they are (Hofstadter 1965). We are able to proceed to their statement or demonstration only because of some earlier moment of our knowing them. Things as they are must, on pain of ceasing to exist, be already partially revealed. This is what I take Heidegger (1971) to mean by *a-lethia*:

Not only must that in conformity with which a cognition orders itself be already in some way unconcealed. The entire *realm* in which this 'conformity to something' goes on must already occur as a whole in the unconcealed ... With all our correct representations we would get nowhere, we could not even pre-suppose that there is already manifest

something to which we can conform ourselves, unless the unconcealed-
ness of beings had already exposed us to, placed us in, that lighted
realm in which every being stands for us and from which it withdraws.

(Heidegger 1971: 52)

Verification stands in relation to validation as does understanding to explanation. Validation, then, is a gloss on verification; or, in Husserlian terms, it
is the provision of other *noemata*, of which abundance may yet avoid the
thing itself. Attention to validation is in effect an attention to method at the
expense of attending to the object which the method should reveal.

Now, returning to the moment of characterization, we can see that if
inquirers stand in relation to their objects in the light of what Hofstadter
(1965) has called 'truth of spirit', then our response to their work – to their
objects, that is – is a *moment of verification*, defined now as *a-letheia*, or un-
hiddenness. The instructive case is that of art. 'Truth of spirit' is the truth
that a thing *is* in order that it *can be* that thing, and is declared by the work
of art's *own* intentionalistic structure. The correlative structure of aesthetic
appreciation reveals this, for it is our openness to the art-object which allows
its accomplishment in our experience, not our projection of it as it ought to
be. However, such aesthetic attending is not a special or marginal case peculiar to artists or their (sophisticated) audiences, but one which can be
systematically developed by them because it is the very foundation of intelligence. This is to say no more than that we attend primarily to objects in
this way as a condition of our being in the world. But in daily experience,
truth of spirit is so unconsciously a mode in which we proceed that it is
occluded by a concern with the more patent and accountable forms of truth
given with intellectual or material schemes. This is still more the case with
the research attitude which, predicated on scientific principles, is methodologically opposed to art in its concern with explicitation. Verification
cannot be a method in this way, failing which it becomes an instrument very
much like validation. For although directed at objects, verification is reflexive in that it asks whether those objects are entertained in a fashion which is
true to their nature, and it can only try this conclusion against its own
experience of those objects. Verification so illuminates the moment of
characterization – the 'original bestowal of meaning' – that it returns the
observer to the objects so constituted.

Thus the criterial questions which attend verification are:

- Is the inquiry object directed?
- Does it seek to know those objects better?
- What does it use to do this?
- Does it reveal the value which prompts and maintains it?

And chiefly,

- How can I know the answers to these questions?

Social research thus becomes first the search for a form within which the answers to all these questions will be coherent. But what medium can bear such a moral charge? What follows is a sketch suggesting some of the ways in which social science research may exploit the expressive character of language through the use of fictional methods.

Fiction and social research: a sketch

Hermeneutics concerns the conditions necessary to interpretation, and is based on the assumption that understanding is linguistic, since it holds the real to be linguistically constituted, and our involvement reflexive. In *The New Hermeneutic*, Murray (1978) develops Heidegger's concept of the 'hermeneutic circle'. There is always first an *interpreter*, for 'only in the context of the existing interpreter can the being of the work matter or make sense' (Murray 1978: 107). The social bonds which interpreter and text share in their common language are described by the *life-relation of the interpreter*. The *pre-understanding of the interpreter* describes how the reader's foreknowledge is brought to anticipation of the text. This meets the essence of that which is interpreted and is 'the particular kind of reality which is experienced in the act of interpretation', constitutive of the text. But,

> literary interpretation not only questions the work; the work also questions the one who understands. The circularity of the interpretative process lies in the movement of questioning and being questioned.
> (Murray 1978: 107–8)

So, finally, the *truth of what is interpreted* is a dialogue with self. 'Each factor', says Murray (1978: 108), 'emerges through making explicit what is involved in the preceding one', and the circle is joined when the truth of the work qualifies the experience of the interpreter.

Historically speaking, the science of hermeneutics belongs to the world of literary texts, and originally to biblical study. But it is clear that as a description of engagement with objects, the hermeneutic circle may describe the more general process of experience, as well as the more specific one of phenomenological research. Metaphorically, then, we could see any situation of objects as a text for interpretation by researchers; their report will be hermeneutic if it tries to explicate their circular involvement with their objects. Our response to their work is similarly circular. So if verification can be said to describe the intuition of the object, we can see that it is properly a hermeneutic moment.

How does such a view of research differ from what is characteristic of the research attitude? In minimizing the involvement of consciousness in the making of knowledge, science in one move suspends the operation of the hermeneutic circle, ignores the linguistic constitution of reality and so immures itself from its objects and from morality. This creates the antinomy of explanation and interpretation which Dilthey (1977) established as exclusive. But Ricoeur (1978) shows that they are in fact continuous moments of the same process of understanding, explanation being a refinement for the sake of communicability. Scientific facts are not moments in a different circle, but events which have been sanitized by a research technology so that the 'original bestowal of meaning' is no longer visible. Medawar (1969: 48), himself a biologist, says that the scientific paper 'glosses and edits all you can actually need to know to replicate the process of discovery'. Not only is this process not the methodologically clean one it is popularly supposed to be, but also it uses linguistic rather than mathematical structures. Medawar tells of biologists in a particular experiment who ask repeatedly of their data 'Does it tell a story?'

Narrative 'man'

Freudian psychoanalysis, for example, is a hermeneutic whose aim is to discover with patients the 'texts' of their lives, and so to teach them the language of their experience. It is Kermode's (1975: 184) view that Freud's research into dreams was so aimed at 'formulating principles applicable to the larger class that contains all narrative discourse'. This 'larger class' is surely described by the narrative form which the intentional structure of consciousness provides around itself. Similarly, according to Sartre, man is always telling stories; it is narrative which gives coherence over time to the field which the 'intentional arc' (of Merleau-Ponty) inhabits. Narrative is not, then, exclusively a property of fiction, but because consciousness shares this structure with it, fiction may have a similarly privileged access to the real. Butor (1979) recognizes this relationship, and claims for the novel in particular a profoundly heuristic function; the novel, he says, is itself a search for form, and study of this form

> allows us to rediscover beyond this fixed narrative everything it camouflages or passes over in silence: that fundamental narrative in which our whole life is steeped.
>
> (Butor 1979: 46)

I earlier characterized all research as search for form; if the novel is similarly charged with describing reality, it is worth exploring what we can learn from its method. Scholes and Kellog (1966: 13) have described two main and antithetical modes of narrative; the *empirical*, which has 'a primary allegiance to the real', is realized by the *historical* account, true to fact, or else by the *mimetic*, which is true to experience; the other mode, the *fictional*, has 'its allegiance to the ideal' and its forms are *romantic*, 'which cultivates beauty and aims to delight', and the *allegorical*, which 'cultivates goodness and aims to instruct'. It is immediately clear that the novel can have any of these forms, and has done so in keeping with developments in human knowledge. The realistic novel had an objective correlate which words hence pointed to; but developments in psychology, particularly, have led writers to a 'fictional' rather than 'empirical' mode whose referent is 'in' consciousness if it can be said to be anywhere at all. Lodge writes:

> The mimetic impulse towards the characterisation of the inner life dissolves inevitably into mythic and expressionistic patterns upon reaching the citadel of the psyche.
>
> (Lodge 1971: 87)

Murdoch (1978: 122) similarly reports one of the dominant twentieth-century forms of the novel as 'crystalline', 'a small quasi-allegorical object portraying the human condition and not containing characters in the nineteenth century sense'.

Reference, if it is allowed, is thus turned in on the lexical surface of the text, and the reader's attention is dominated not by referents or plot, say, but by some internally rhythmic system of the composition. In the extreme Barthean account (Barthes 1975), characters become collections of *semes* – such as honesty, wit, and so on – which attach to names. Where writers once wrote to address a single, realistic, perceptual world, they now increasingly give up this 'reality' in the attempt to find the mythical, symbolic, archetypical structures behind individual experience.

But paradoxically, these allegorical and fragmenting forms are attempts at a better, truer empirical form. These developments are not simply literary responses to a field opened up by psychology and linguistics and anthropology; they are, as Malraux (1949: 81) says of style, 'a call for and not a consequence of a way of seeing'. What they innovate is reality itself. The novel is a search for the form which can carry the weight of its ever-unfolding insight, and the novelist's obligation

> is to make himself a stylistic and experiential citizen of a world that does not fully exist for him until he has done this; he has to invent the possibility of a book in a world he sees as not yet fully named.
>
> (Bradbury 1978: 7)

But it is Butor (1979) more than anyone who insists on the moral and heuristic character of the novel, and through whose work we can begin to see its contiguity with social research generally. In the following passage he might well be talking of the research-worker:

> The novelist who refuses to accept this task (of 'unmasking, exploration, and adaptation'), never discarding old habits, never demanding any particular effort of his reader, never obliging him to confront

himself, to question attitudes long since taken for granted . . . becomes the accomplice of that profound uneasiness, that darkness, in which we are groping our way. He stiffens the reflexes of our consciousness even more, making any awakening more difficult; he contributes to its suffocation, so that even if his intentions are generous, his work is in the last analysis a poison.

(Butor 1979: 48)

And one could similarly substitute 'research' for 'the novel' in his conclusion:

Formal invention in the novel, far from being opposed to realism as shortsighted critics often assume, is the *sine qua non* of a greater realism.

(Butor 1979: 48)

'A call for a way of seeing'

What might persuade us that we have returned to talk of research is the sense of responsibility towards their matter which researchers should share with the novelist, and the criterion of truth-to-things with which we appreciate a work. In the case of the novel as with the moral social research, the 'original bestowal of meaning' arises from the ground of reality, and generates an intentional appraisal of those objects which liberates consciousness from its previous, less particular way of holding them. Conversely, the worst of research is just like the form of those novels which

give us an image of reality in flagrant contradiction to the reality which gave them birth and which they are concerned to pass over in silence. They are impostures which it is the duty of criticism to expose; for such work, for all their charm and merits, preserve and deepen the darkness, imprison consciousness in its contradictions, in its blindness, which risks leading it into the most fatal disorders.

(Butor 1979: 50)

But, pitched against the status quo of the novel – or of standardized 'safe' research methods – writers have the task of delivering their work from its 'original bestowal of meaning', while the objects of this bestowal remain our only test of its rightness. Lodge (1971) describes the dynamic of this essentially rhetorical problem:

In the novel personal experience must be explored and transmuted until it acquires an authenticity and persuasivness independent of its actual origin; while the fictive imagination through which this exploration and transmutation is achieved is itself subject to an empirical standard of accuracy and plausibility.

(Lodge 1971: 108)

The text becomes a witness of that dynamic for it 'lives' for the reader between the finite statements it presents lexically, and the infinite experience of the reader, which verifies them. But if texts are ever open to new integrations, it is mistaken to suppose that they are merely 'like a picnic, to which the author brings the words and the reader the meaning' (Frye 1957). The correlate of the author's responsibility is just that of the reader, and if the novelist creates their characters – as Thackeray said – by 'consulting' them, then the reader must do the same. We may no longer identify the meaning of a text with its *mens autoris* but, as Johnson (1978) points out, authors take care with words because they have a precise job for those words to do, and which fails or is frustrated if they rather license for the reader something other than what the text – as the author's agent – requires and provides. But there remains an area of negotiation because the text is self-consciously distinct from 'the thing', and because appreciation must be coherent within personal experience. It is for reasons like this that Butor (1979: 46) calls the novel 'the phenomenological realm *par excellence*, the best possible place to study how reality appears to us or might appear'. And it is because there is such an intentional space between entropy and redundancy – a breach in intersubjectivity – that hermeneutics establishes itself as the science of involvement with a text.

The novel stands as all of a form, a metaphor and a model of research. As a form, its wholly linguistic character suggests its moral commitment to the reader's experience, without which its life is limited; as a metaphor for research it chiefly emphasizes the urge to present veracious narrative; as a model it combines these virtues to show how the definition of reality is essentially a linguistic and therefore cooperative activity, directed at objects which it can never exhaust. But it is mainly as a form that it is valuable because given with its form is the obligation to *search for form*, failing which it can have nothing to say.

The scheme above does not easily translate either into the jargon of a current critique of educational research, or into the language of the handbook of research methods. But I believe that it indicates some of the conceptual tools that are needed to enable researchers – and particularly teachers and other researchers of educational settings (Convey 1993; Campbell 2000) – to transform the means of educational research production into events with radical outcomes which can dissolve once and for all meaningless oppositions like 'theory' and 'practice'. In particular, the capacity of story for 'validating the interconnectedness of the past, the present, the future, the personal and the professional in an educator's life' (Beattie 1995: 54) is immense and powerful. Such work has an unavoidable moral urgency in a period of educational practices set about with the furniture of audit. 'Any approach,' Michael Apple reminds us, 'that evacuates the aesthetic, the personal and the ethical from our activities as educators is not about education at all' (Apple 1996: xiii; see also Coffey 1999).

The point was made forcefully by Fred Inglis in the late 1960s:

Such research has no utilitarian justification; it cannot provide incontrovertible data for prediction. It justifies itself more as a map on which many individuals may find their place. Like a novel, it gives readers . . . a chance to recognise themselves, and to do this it needs to realise that 'subtle interrelatedness' (in D.H. Lawrence's phrase) which marks creative fiction. It needs, therefore, to attempt a realisation of a total context, and intellectual and moral milieu, and any such attempt will only make sense as there is present in the writing without self-importance or self-consciousness the personality of the writer himself.

(Inglis 1969: 15)

Thus with such a position it becomes possible to conduct research and/or tell stories of educational settings which bear immediate relation to the truths from which they derive. Such research acts become matters of urgency, for they test the moral and political intent of the researcher (and of the reader). The challenge then is to approach the crises of representation with accounts which embody the truths of those situations – as they are read – and without recourse to methodological *apologia*.

References

Apple, M. (1996) *Cultural Politics and Education*. Buckingham: Open University Press.

Bacon, W.A. (1979) *The Art of Interpretation*, 3rd edn. New York: Holt, Rinehart and Winston.

Barone, T. (1998) Persuasive writings, vigilant readings and reconstructed characters: the paradox of trust in educational storytelling, in J. Hatch and R. Wisniewski (eds) *Life History and Narrative*. London: Falmer.

Barthes, R. (1975) *Roland Barthes par Roland Barthes*. Paris: Seuil.

Beattie, M. (1995) New prospects for teacher education: narrative ways of knowing teacher and teacher learning, *Educational Research*, 37(1): 53–70.

Becker, H.S., McCall, M.M. and Morris, L.V. (1989) Theatres and communities: three scenes, *Social Problems*, 36: 93–116.

Berger, J. (1996) *Photocopies*. London: Bloomsbury.

Bolton, N. (1981) Research and change. Unpublished paper, University of Sheffield.

Booth, T. (1996) Sounds of still voices: issues in the use of narrative methods with people who have learning difficulties, in L. Barton (ed.) *Sociology and Disability: Some Emerging Issues*. London: Longman.

Bradbury, M. (1978) *The Novel Today*. Manchester: Manchester University Press.

Bridges, D. (1998) Research, dissent and the reinstatement of theory, in J. Rudduck and D. McIntyre (eds) *Challenges for Educational Research*. London: Paul Chapman.

Burgess R. (ed.) (1985) *Strategies of Educational Research: Qualitative Methods*. Milton Keynes: Open University Press.

Butor, M. (1979) *Inventory: Essays*. London: Cape.

Campbell, A. (2000) Fictionalising research data as a way of increasing teacher's access to school-focused research, *Research in Education*, 63 (May): 81–8.

Carr, W. and Kemmis, S. (1986) *Becoming Critical: Education, Knowledge and Action Research*. Falmer: Lewes.

Clough, P. (1995) Problems of identity and method in the investigation of special educational needs, in P. Clough and L. Barton (eds) *Making Difficulties: Research and the Construction of Special Educational Needs*. London: Paul Chapman.

Clough, P. (1996) 'Again fathers and sons': the mutual construction of self, story and special educational needs, *Disability and Society*, 11(1): 71–81.

Clough, P. (1998) Differently articulate? Some indices of disturbed/disturbing voices, in P. Clough and L. Barton (eds) *Articulating with Difficulty: Research Voices in Inclusive Education*. London: Paul Chapman and Sage.

Clough, P. (1999) Crises of schooling and the 'crisis of representation': the story of Rob, *Qualitative Inquiry*, 5(3): 428–48.

Clough, P. and Barton, L. (eds) (1995) *Making Difficulties: Research and the Construction of Special Educational Needs*. London: Paul Chapman.

Clough, P. and Corbett, J. (2000) *Theories of Inclusive Education*. London: PCP/Sage.

Coates, J. (1986) *Women, Men and Language*. London: Longman.

Coffey, A. (1999) *The Ethnographic Self: Fieldwork and the Representation of Identity*. London: Sage.

Convey, A. (1993) Developing fictional writing as a means of stimulating teacher reflection: a case study, *Educational Action Research*, 1: 135–52.

Crotty, M. (1998) *The Foundations of Social Research*. London: Sage.

Davie, R., Upton, G. and Varma, V. (eds) (1996) *The Voice of the Child*. London: Falmer.

Denzin, N. (1989) *Interpretive Interactionism*. Newbury Park, CA: Sage.

Denzin, N.K. (1997) *Interpretive Ethnography: Ethnographic Practices for the 21st Century*. London: Sage.

Denzin, N. and Lincoln, Y. (eds) (2000) *Handbook of Qualitative Methods in Educational Enquiry*. London: Sage.

DfEE (1997a) *Excellence in Schools*. London: The Stationery Office.

DfEE (1997b) Press release number 442/97, 30 December.

DfEE (1998) *The National Literacy Strategy: Framework for Teaching*. London: DfEE.

Didion, I. (1968) *Slouching Towards Bethlehem*. New York: Farrar.

Dilthey, W. (1977) *Descriptive Psychology and Historical Understanding*. The Hague: Nijhoff.

Dyson, A. (1998) Professional intellectuals from powerful groups: wrong from the start?, in P. Clough and L. Barton (eds) *Articulating with Difficulty: Research Voices in Inclusive Education*. London: PCP/Sage.

Erben, M. (ed.) (1998) *Biography and Education: A Reader*. London: Falmer.

Frater, D. (1997) *Improving Boys' Literacy*. London: Basic Skills Agency.

Frye, N. (1957) *Anatomy of Criticism*. Princeton, NJ: Princeton University Press.

Gardiner, J. (1997) Blunkett to continue 'shaming', *Times Educational Supplement*, 14 November.

Geertz, C. (1988) *Works and Lives: The Anthropologist as Author*. Stanford, CA: Stanford University Press.

Giddens, A. (1991) *Modernity and Self-Identity*. Cambridge: Polity.

Glaser, B.J. and Strauss, A.L. (1967) *The Discovery of Grounded Theory: Strategies for Qualitative Research*. Chicago: Aldine.

Goodson, I. and Sikes, P. (2001) *Life History Research in Educational Settings*. Buckingham: Open University Press.

Hamilton, D. (1998) The silence of the shadows: educational research and the ESRC, in J. Rudduck and D. McIntyre (eds) *Challenges for Educational Research*. London: Paul Chapman.

Hargreaves, D.H. (1997) In defence of research for evidence-based teaching: a rejoinder to Martyn Hammersley, *British Educational Research Journal*, 23: 405–20.

Hatch, J. and Wisniewski, R. (eds) (1998) *Life History and Narrative*. London: Falmer.

Haydon, D. (1997) Crisis in the classroom, in P. Scraton (ed.) *'Childhood' in 'Crisis'?* London: UCL Press.

Heidegger, M. (1962) *Being and Time*. London: SCM Press.

Heidegger, M. (1971) *Poetry, Language and Thought*. New York: Harper and Row.

Hofstadter, A. (1965) *Truth and Art*. New York: Columbia University Press.

hooks, bell (1991) Narratives of struggle, in P. Mariani (ed.) *Critical Fictions: The Politics of Imaginative Writing*. Seattle, WA: Bay Press.

Husserl, E. (1960) *Cartesian Meditations*. The Hague: Nijhoff.

Husserl, E. (1970) *The Crisis of European Sciences and Transcendental Phenomenology*, trans. D. Carr. Evanston, IL: Northwestern University Press.

Hutton-Jarvis, C. (1999) Text or testament? A comparison of educational and literary critical approaches to research, *Qualitative Studies in Education*, 12(6): 659–70.

Inglis, F. (1969) *The Englishness of English Teaching*. London: Longman.

Johnson, B.S. (1978) Introduction to 'Aren't you rather young to be writing your memoirs?', in M. Bradbury *The Novel Today*. Manchester: Manchester University Press.

Kermode, F. (1975) *How We Read Novels*. London: Routledge and Kegan Paul.

Kuhn, T. (1970) *The Structure of Scientific Revolutions*, 2nd edn. Chicago: University of Chicago Press.

Lather, P. and Smithies, C. (1997) *Troubling the Angels: Women Living with HIV/AIDS*. Boulder, CO: Westview.

Lincoln, Y. (1995) The sixth moment: emerging problems in qualitative research, *Studies in Symbolic Interaction*, 19: 37–55.

Lodge, D. (1971) *The Novelist at the Crossroads*. London: Routledge.

MacIntyre, A. (1985) *After Virtue: A Study in Moral Theory*, 2nd edn. London: Duckworth.

McLeod, J. (1997) *Narrative and Psychotherapy*. London: Sage.

MacMurray, J. (1935) *Reason and Emotion*. London: Faber and Faber.

Mahony, P. (1985) *Schools for the Boys*. London: Hutchinson.

Malraux, A. (1949) *The Psychology of Art*. London: Zwemmer.

Mansell, W. (2000) Inquests link four deaths to inspection, *Times Educational Supplement*, 21 April.

Marcus, G.E. (1994) What comes (just) after 'Post'? The case of ethnography, in N.K. Denzin and Y.S. Lincoln (eds) *The Handbook of Qualitative Research*. Thousand Oaks, CA: Sage.

Medawar, P. (1969) *The Art of the Soluble*. Harmondsworth: Penguin.

Meiners, E.R. (1999) Writing (of) fragments, *Qualitative Studies in Education*, 12(4): 347–62.

Mendick, R. (1998) Crushed under the wheels of OFSTED, *Times Educational Supplement*, 4 December.

Merleau-Ponty, M. (1962) *Phenomenology of Perception*. London: Routledge.

Mink, L. (1978) Narrative form as a cognitive instrument, in R.H. Canary and H. Kozicki (eds) *The Writing of History: Literary Form and Historical Understanding*. Madison, WI: University of Wisconsin Press.

Morrison, B. (1996) Introduction to A. Burgess (1962) *A Clockwork Orange*. Harmondsworth: Penguin.

Murdoch, I. (1978) Against dryness, in M. Bradbury *The Novel Today*. Manchester: Manchester University Press.

Murray, M. (1978) *The New Hermeneutic*. London: Routledge and Kegan Paul.

Nayak, A. and Kehily, M.J. (1996) Playing it straight: masculinities, homophobias and schooling, *Journal of Gender Studies*, 5(2): 24–36.

Oakeshott, M. (1933) *Experience and its Modes*. Cambridge: Cambridge University Press.

Passmore, B. (2000) From Tibet relief to Teacherline, *Times Educational Supplement*, 7 April.

Picasso, P. (1923) Picasso speaks, *The Arts*, May: 5.

Postman, N. (1992) *Technopoly: The Surrender of Culture to Technology*. New York: Knopf.

Pring, R. (2000) *Philosophy of Educational Research*. London: Continuum.

Prosser, J. (ed.) (1998) *Image-based Research: A Source Book for Qualitative Researchers*. London: Falmer.

Pyke, N. (1998) 'Unjust' OFSTED drove head from job, *Times Educational Supplement*, 29 May.

Rafferty, F., Dean, C. and Rowinski, P. (1998) Labour gives up shaming schools, *Times Educational Supplement*, 2 October.

Richardson, L. (1994) Writing: a method of inquiry, in N.K. Denzin and Y.S. Lincoln (eds) *Handbook of Qualitative Research*. Thousand Oaks, CA: Sage.

Ricoeur, P. (1978) *The Philosophy of Paul Ricoeur*. Boston, MA: Beacon.

Riseborough, G. (1993) GBH: the Gobbo Barmy Harmy, in I. Bates and G. Riseborough (eds) *Youth and Inequality*. Buckingham: Open University Press.

Rorty, R. (1989) *Contingency, Irony and Solidarity*. Cambridge: Cambridge University Press.

Rosen, H. (2000) *Speaking from Memory: The Study of Autobiographical Discourse*. Stoke-on-Trent: Trentham.

Sandelowski, M. (1994) The proof is in the pottery: towards a poetic for qualitative enquiry, in J. Morse (ed.) *Critical Issues in Qualitative Research Methods*. London: Sage.

Scholes, R. and Kellog, R. (1966) *The Nature of Narrative*. New York: Open University Press.

School Curriculum and Assessment Authority (SCAA) (1997) *Boys and English*. London: SCAA.

Skelton, C. (1996) Learning to be tough: the fostering of maleness in one primary school, *Gender and Education*, 8(2): 185–97.

Sparkes, A. (1994) Life histories and the issue of voice: reflections on an 'emerging relationship', *International Journal of Qualitative Studies in Education*, 7: 165–83.

St Pierre, E.A. (1997) Methodology in the fold and the irruption of transgressive data, *International Journal of Qualitative Studies in Education*, 10(2): 175–89.

Stevens, W. (1965) *Selected Poems*. London: Faber and Faber.

Stronach, I. and MacLure, M. (1998) *Educational Research Undone*. London: Routledge.

Swann, J. (1992) *Girls, Boys and Language*. Oxford: Blackwell.

Tierney, W.G. (1995) (Re)presentation and voice, *Qualitative Inquiry*, 1(4): 379–90.

Tierney, W.G. (1998) Life history's history: subjects foretold, *Qualitative Inquiry*, 4(1): 49–70.

Tooley, J. (1998) *Educational Research: A Critique*. London: Ofsted.

Trinh T. Minh-ha (1991) *When the Moon Waxes Red: Representation, Gender and Cultural Politics*. New York: Routledge.

Vulliamy, G. and Webb, R. (eds) (1992) *Teacher Research and Special Educational Needs*. London: David Fulton.

Walford, G. (1991) *Doing Educational Research*. London: Routledge.

Whitehead, A.N. (1948) *Essays in Science and Philosophy*. New York: Rider.

Williams, R. (1969) *The Long Revolution*. Harmondsworth: Penguin.

Wiltshire Education Support and Training (1996) *Boys and English*. Swindon: Wiltshire County Council.

Winterson, J. (1991) *Oranges are Not the Only Fruit*. London: Vantage.

Yalom, D. (1991) *Love's Executioner: And Other Tales of Psychotherapy*. Harmondsworth: Penguin.

| Index